Ink in the Wheels:
Stories to Make Love Roll

Megan M Cutter

D1127892

Ink in the Wheels:
Stories to Make Love Roll

S. BARTON & MEGAN M. CUTTER

Foreword by
P.J. DIXON

Cutter's Edge Consulting

Cutter's Edge Consulting, LLC
Raleigh, NC

Megan M. Cutter
megan@cuttersedgeconsulting.com
S. Barton Cutter
barton@cuttersedgeconsulting.com

For more information:
Cutter's Edge Consulting, LLC
www.cuttersedgeconsulting.com

Library of Congress Cataloging-in-Publication Control # 2012953481

ISBN # 978-1-4675-4459-7

Printed in the United States of America

*This is a true story of actual events in the life of
Megan M. Cutter and S. Barton Cutter from their own perspectives.
The authors make no warranties, expressed or implied,
with respect to the completeness of accuracy of the information
contained herein.*

*Immediate family members mentioned have signed official permissions
of use within the book. Other names have been changed to protect their
individual privacy.*

*S. Barton Cutter and Megan M. Cutter do not provide individual relationship
advice. Their professional coaching and mentorship services are delivered
on a best effort basis. Cutter's Edge Consulting, LLC, S. Barton and Megan
M. Cutter are not liable for the outcomes of relationships nor are they liable
for individual decisions or actions taken by individuals in the relationship
who read this manuscript.*

Our journey together is etched in
wheelchair tracks,
Carved by laughter and love; these are
the stories of our lives.
We dedicate our story
to other couples on their own journey,
those who are still looking
and those who do not yet believe
they can find.
For one day,
we will each grow out of our shells
and discover the courage to make
life our own.

~ S. Barton and Megan M. Cutter

CONTENTS

Ink in the Wheels:
Stories to Make Love Roll

Two pebbles fumbling
into lapis water.
Wakes massage
like kneading paws upon the shore.
The sky shimmers turquoise stars,
their rays weaving the mosaic of the web.

~Barton and Megan Cutter, September 2004

Acknowledgment

The process of writing and publishing the book could not be made without a gathering of supporters who have encouraged, inspired, and motivated us to tell our story and give others that spark that keeps us moving beyond what we think is possible. There are so many who have given us strength and courage along the way.

To our editor, Satia Renée who has done an amazing job asking us the right questions to polish and fine tune every word. To Elizabeth Galecke of Elizabeth Galecke Photography for her amazing photography that beautifully illustrated the full expression of our relationship. To Cyn Macgregor of Cynergie Studio for her artful design of the cover and interior layout. And to our publicist Diana Ennen, for helping us reach and impact individuals, families, professionals, and community leaders around the world. To Drew Becker of Convey Media Group and Shane Dittmar, who made the book trailer possible—we thank you all!

In unending gratitude of those who have taken us over the edge of what we thought was possible: Helen House, who gave Megan insight into discovering clarity and focus, while blazing her own path and revealing once again the depth of impact we have on others; Ken Mossman, whose profound coaching has illumined Barton's inner-monkey and unlocked in him the courage to howl with laughter; and Phil Okrend, who fostered the beginning of an amazing journey to explore the dynamics of our relationship in a new way and the belief in our ability to achieve our dreams.

For those who have known us since the beginning: Mindy, Eric & the boys, Penny & Mike, P.J., Jennifer, Robert, Karl & Carol, and many of our other brothers and sisters—for lighting the fire that keeps us going and who inspire us to let our sparks light the way for others.

We give many thanks to our local community and neighbors for your support over the years: Sloan Meek, whose fearless and bold spirit rocks on in exploration of profound creativity; the Triangle Area Freelancers and Alice Osborn for continued camaraderie and support; Jacqueline Cavadi; for mentoring Barton and taking him under your wing; Holly Riddle for sharing Barton's pickiness for words; Nancy Stolfo-Corti who wrote her own truth and supported us in doing the same; Donna Hedgepeth for your unending work with families and for your friendship; along with so many others who have been a part of our journey.

Publishing this manuscript could not have been possible without so many supporters! We would like to give a huge thank you and tell the world how wonderful these supporters are: Stan Cutter, Catherine Cutter, Howard Lickerman, David Lickerman, George and Ellen Aman, Adam Maclennan, Mary Catherine Plunkett, Helen House, Henry and Karen Kimsey-House, Janet Perlstein, Carolyn Baxley, Steven and Angela Potts, Sean MacBain, Kimberly Kirchstein, Kate Roeske-Zummer, Pamela Knight Mattsson, Jeff Jacobson, Beth Shapiro, and many others that are not named here.

A special thank you to our families who have watched and supported us as we have grown, struggled, fallen, risen, and thrived over these years—Stan and Nancy, Catherine, Andrew and Lauren, Louis and Linda, Scott, and Beth. And in loving memory of Megan's mother, Anna. To all our extended family members for your love, support and encouragement.

Above all, we'd like to thank our clients, students, and all we serve for what you have taught us, for keeping us on track, and for being brave and courageous.

Foreword

Being asked to write the Foreword of anyone's book is an incredible honor and, according to Google and Wikipedia, fairly important—most research said, *it was MY job to inspire people to read on.*

So as I began writing this Foreword—in hopes of doing my job and inspiring you to continue reading—I was immediately reminded of the opening scene in the movie, The Princess Bride, when the sick boy's grandfather shows up and brings him a book, and the boy asks him if there are any sports in it.

The Grandfather says, "Are you kidding? Fencing, fighting, torture, revenge, giants, monsters, chases, escapes, true love, miracles . . ."

Well, that's how I felt as I was reading through Ink in the Wheels; it has everything—there's adventure, romance, humor, narrow escapes, tumultuous encounters, tragedy, inspiration, and even sex—oh yes, I did say "sex;" and now that I have your attention, allow me to introduce two people, who's story is well worth reading: Barton and Megan Cutter.

I have known Barton for nearly 14 years and, in that time, I can honestly say he has been one of my greatest heroes! His heart is unwavering and unconditional in his love, support, and gratitude for people; as a result, everyone who meets him, . . . loves, respects, admires, and appreciates him. Personally, I consider myself incredibly fortunate to be friends with such an outstanding human being.

Although Megan and I have never met face-to-face, her story of their first encounter and the love she shares with one of my dearest friends drew me to tears quite often. Megan, . . . Thank You, *I Love Love*, and I sincerely appreciate you for embracing my friend so completely!

Ink in the Wheels is a beautiful, and fascinating, account of their love. Their story leaves nothing out—touching on the physical, psychological, emotional, spiritual, even financial. These two have life long aspirations and the necessary motivation, drive, and supportive partnership to propel themselves—and everyone they come in contact with—into a state of profound change.

Nothing holds them back as they embrace challenges together and actively explore options and alternatives for overcoming obstacles.

As I was reading this book, I found myself continually impressed at their amazing honesty and frankness; it's the candor of revealing everything so freely that exudes a certain kind of unparalleled courage and charisma—leaving everyone who reads their story inspired and thoroughly impressed.

Barton's writings conjure brilliant imagery and evoke the reader's imagination, curiosity, and emotional commitment to the story at every step of their shared journey. And Megan writes with sincere passion, filling every sentence with such raw, honest emotion that I often felt a lump welling up in my throat and tears rising in my eyes as I read her words. They both have captivating writing styles, and I personally appreciated their skill of packing every sentence with emotionally-rich content and expression.

I've never made it through a wedding without crying and, although I wasn't actually at Megan and Barton's wedding, . . . this wedding—in their book—is no different. As I read the individual renditions of their wedding day memories, I found myself in near constant tears, as the sheer beauty of their love persevered, despite seemingly insur-mountable odds.

With complete confidence, I say this was truly one of the most beau-tiful weddings ever beheld by hearts and eyes; their love is palpable, ... *even in their writings.*

Speaking of the palpability of love, this book is riddled with the exquisite poetry of two clearly impassioned lovers, leaving me to believe their next literary collaboration will be a book of erotic love poems. Their prose are rich beyond measure and may very well steal the show in some cases—*they are oh so sensual*—like the crystalline sugars of a single, sweet melon melting into your tongue, juicy and tactilely-delicious; the same sense occurs emotionally, as we drink in the words of their poetic and, often, provocative language. All human beings should be so blessed to have someone so profoundly to love, and in love with them.

Every chapter, of course, tells a different story, but one thread of commonality throughout most of the book is Barton's easy going approach to life, which is incredibly refreshing; I truly wish everyone was as easy about life and the misadventures we often find ourselves in as he is—maybe it's because he often finds himself in oddly unusual, and often potentially harrowing, situations that allows him to approach life with such an easy and carefree attitude.

When Barton tells you a story, you can almost count on something bordering on a near life-and-death experience happening to him—so far they've all ended well, *thank goodness*! All these tales typically have two things in common; 1.) the audience, or reader in this book's case, inevitably sit on the edge of their seats, open mouthed, and concerned for Barton's safety—even though he sits before them *recalling* his near harrowing experience. And 2.) very nearly every single story I've ever heard Barton tell ends with him hysterically laughing at himself—and anyone who knows Barton, or has been in his presence during one of these fits of gregarious laughter, knows Barton to have *THE MOST* contagious laugh ever!

In fact, as I write this, I find myself smiling and chuckling at his natural and untamed expression of happiness; he smiles this perfect smile—one of pure, pure joy—eyes sparkling, body convulsing with muscular spasticity and, inevitably, he gives way to this *wonderful* laugh you can feel with more than just your funny bone; you sincerely feel it coursing throughout your body and coming to rest fully in your heart.

Barton's laugh and smile alone could bring World Peace—*anyone who knows him knows this to be an undeniably true statement!*

His antics and misadventures, on the other hand, could bring his loving and beautiful wife to an early grave. Poor Megan—so brave, yet so wrought with undue stress at her husband's mishaps and escapades; I imagine every time he leaves the house, she wonders what kind of folly he'll find himself in today (if he's not careful); and for Barton, ... *these crazy exploits are just a part of every day life.*

For what it's worth, I'm a big superhero fan—doing the right thing, even when it's hard; overcoming seemingly insurmountable odds; even offering evil-doers a second chance to repent before being banished "forever"—these characteristics almost always inspire me and bring me to tears. And, although, I'm a man, I'm not ashamed to say I cry, as you know already, at how Megan's story throughout this book has touched me.

In many ways, I see Megan as a superhero, too; obviously I don't mean I see her running around in spandex and tights, tying people up with her magic lasso—well, I might, but I don't think Barton would be too fond of that image rolling around in my head—so I suppose the whole lasso-and-tights fantasy might be better left to the lovers.

Seriously though, if there's any kind of super powers attributed to anyone in this book, it would have to be to Megan. She has obviously persevered through unfortunate rejection, the tragedy of loss, judgment, disappointment, and resistance—and surprisingly gracefully too. In martial arts, we might refer to these kinds of situations as multiple attacker scenarios, and one of the most important things to practice in these types of encounters is to *keep moving*!

Megan has expertly navigated these events in her life by utilizing wisdom, intellect, and integrity, coupled with her two greatest super powers: perseverance and persistence; simply put—*Megan NEVER quits*!

It's this fierce determination that Megan has used to rise above obstacles throughout her life, pulling herself out of the fire of suffering—every time—like the Phoenix, rising from the ashes of "certain" death. Life might not have always been easy for her; however, I'm confident, she'd say it's been worth it.

This beautiful woman—wife, lover, and business partner—has done an incredible job defining the value her husband seems to consistently bring into her life, which is important for other couples when we remember they are engaged in an inter-ability relationship; this book is far more than the story of their love, it's a guide for couples of all kinds to succeed, despite the odds and resistance against them.

Megan and Barton's life together seems to be one of the great love stories of our time. I thoroughly enjoyed how Megan, throughout the book, reveals her love, respect, and appreciation for her husband—an element of such importance within healthy relationships; and I find myself even more inspired when I'm reminded—even though I know—*Barton's in a wheelchair!*

The things Megan reveals about Barton show him to hold a standard that far exceeds that of the average man, and he consistently seems to demonstrate an attitude and willingness of real masculinity—despite his disability. All women deserve a gentle, yet masculine partner and all men should strive to be that kind of provider—*if she's not careful, she's going to have all kinds of competition from other women*—for as the quote says, "a boy makes his girl jealous of other women, a true gentleman makes other women jealous of his girl."

I am exceedingly awed, inspired, and proud of both of them! Tenacity is a skill many in the world lack; however, *empowered by divine love and the deepest of integrity, . . . Megan and Barton stand as one* for each other and every one of us. Their message, whether able-bodied or disabled, is clear—the conviction of love is a force more profound than any cognitive conception can truly conceive. If not for the human heart and spirit of unwavering commitment—respect, appreciation, and love could not be tasted, . . . let alone embraced. Megan and my friend, Barton, give hope to romantics everywhere.

Live Free My Beautiful Friends, Live Free!

P.J. Dixon, *Motivational Speaker*

Introduction

When I, Barton, was young, I found that my greatest tool for finding my way through an able-bodied world was my personal willingness to talk about my experience living with a disability and to become vulnerable enough to share my needs with those who surrounded me. Through this process, I came to discover the power of building deeply personal connections with close friends as well as new acquaintances.

I saw their understanding grow along with their ability to relate to people in significantly different situations from their own. I also understood how denying these possible connections through an unwillingness to share reinforced the fears and stereotypes instilled in our culture. I brought this perspective of unapologetic openness to our marriage.

While Barton shared his story from a young age, I, Megan was still discovering my voice and my story, even after we met. Growing up, I hid my notebooks of poetry and stories under the bed, in a closet or school locker in an effort to preserve a genuine sense of myself. I was not used to being so public in terms of my life or needs.

When I met Barton, I was unaware of the transformation that would take place allowing me to vocalize my story and affect others in a profound way. Through sharing the story of our relationship, I realized my own vision of why it was so important to allow others the space to express themselves—through writing, storytelling, or other forms of creative expression.

Neither one of our stories is complete without the other's. Through sharing the story of how we met and live together, we have crossed boundaries and limitations in ways we could not have imagined.

While there is a temptation by many to set us apart as, on the one hand, an unbalanced partnership in which Barton has become a labor of love or an unnecessary burden and, on the other hand, an idealized marriage that rivals any storybook love, the truth is, there is little difference between our relationship and the relationship of any other couple.

What relationship doesn't have discussions over finances, day-to-day logistics, unexpected trips to the emergency room, or even that one doubtful family member whose sole purpose is to cause chaos and discord?

While these pieces of daily life are ever present, they do not represent the core connection between two people. The way we cut through all of the tangles in which we find ourselves is by continually rediscovering the shared vision within the partnership.

Not every inter-ability couple is comfortable with sharing their story or answering questions about their lives. Many couples just want to live their lives without public explanation.

While our own experiences are only a handful among an infinite array of possibilities, we feel that all too often, those who are, work with, and are family members of people with disabilities struggle to reach the point of defining life on their own terms due to an under abundance of successful examples of what life could be like if they dared to dream.

Though there are, within each community, shining examples of those who have broken the mold, all too often parents of children with disabilities find themselves overwhelmed with the unending number of professional opinions: from doctors, from therapists, from educators, and even from well-meaning family members, or friends. Direct support staff members may find themselves caught between wanting to assist their clients in leading independent lives but are limited by funding sources and bureaucracy. And most importantly, those who have disabilities themselves have become acculturated into a system of disempowerment, believing there is no alternative but to accept the status quo.

Our intent for these stories is not to serve as an all-encompassing voice for the dreams, hopes, and desires of people with disabilities, or even a model for how inter-ability relationships ought to function. No. We are each unique, and likewise our relationships to others will express themselves differently, though, the core of what binds them together may be the same. In many ways, we are still figuring it out, just as other inter-ability couples have done.

We offer these stories in service to all who dream of a richer, fuller life. As you read, rather than attempting to emulate the aspects of our journey, look beyond the words to discover the gems that resonate with your own life and open the door to a new definition of what may be possible for you as you navigate each step of your journey.

It is our hope that through these words, those who read it will be inspired and opened by the possibilities that lay within the hearts of each of us, stirred to breathe life into our own potential, and set aside the fears and doubts that limit our soul's freedom.

Grasp the courage to build a life that is truly of your own design.

*At breakfast, you looked into me like a shaft of sun roasting through
the ocean's depths.
Your smile was unvanishing in between nibbles of bagel.
                    I could think only "I love you"*

*and when my lips moistened to speak,
                    no more than a pucker came from them.*

*Your thoughts went back to that day in the living room where the
wafts of sage sparkled like the corner of your eye mid-connection.*

*   Now, I look to calling you wife and dream
that this temporal distance fades between us.*

~ S. Barton Cutter, February 2004

Through the Turquoise Eye

*When tears fall
from the turquoise eye,
lightning tears
through the earth;
We soar free.*

~ S. Barton Cutter, May 2003

The day I returned from camp, I sat calmly outside my Tucson apartment watching a hummingbird dance from bush to bush as storm clouds began to mount overhead. Not only did I find myself in a state of rapture from having finished a week of martial arts training in Sedona, but I also found myself glowing inwardly with delight from an unexpected encounter with an amazing woman.

As the storm drifted southward into the Tucson Valley, I felt comforted by the dancing whispers of lightning as they rumbled across the Catalina Peaks. I knew they were speaking to me, and I hung on every hidden meaning that tore through the sky with an erratic flash. I had no idea what was being asked of me at the time, nor could I ever anticipate where these visions would guide me. Even now, the deep pulse of that afternoon calls me to breathe a love more profound than the brightest perfection of human existence.

As the rain reached the apartments and enlivened the rusted sands beneath my wheels, the heavy drops met my head, words rose from within, and I retired to my room to bear them life. I had seen Megan once before this week at camp. I found her beautiful and was stricken with an uncanny sense of familiarity. Downplaying my immediate attraction to her, I went on about my primary focus of training. During the week at camp, however, it became clear to me that our time together could offer much more than the fleeting sensation of lust.

To my computer I went, pulling the small turquoise stone she had given me, along with her email address from my pocket. I grinned with an innocent delight, and tapped out a quick note along with a verse born of the lightning's inspiration. At the same time, I felt surprisingly unattached to what may or may not happen, trusting only in the feeling of having nothing to lose.

Our email conversations grew richer by the day, as did the outpouring of words. Megan awakened in me an untapped reservoir of the poetic, which poured with the thickness of unrefined syrup. Megan never knew until much later how long the physical act of typing took me, pecking letter by letter with a beak-like pointer strapped to my head. In these hours, I found my aversion to the time-consuming act replaced by a boundless determination to craft the perfect email.

After a month of watching our conversation deepen to the point where I noticed email fall short of the distinct nuances found in the voice, I mustered the courage to call. I must admit, I was greatly relieved when, rather than Megan herself, I was greeted by a recorded message. Yet several minutes later, Megan called me back.

"Hi Barton," Megan's voice rang clearly through the phone.

"Yes?" I choked with excitement as a spasm shot through my body, slamming my upper torso firmly into the back of my wheelchair.

"It's Megan. Sorry I missed your call. I just walked in the door. How are you?"

"I'm great, h-how are you?" forcing the words from my throat, hoping to make myself clear enough to be understood.

"Good. I didn't understand all of your message, but I am so excited to hear your voice."

I asked, "Have you been writing recently?"

"I'm sorry, I didn't quite catch that."

"No problem. I asked have you been writing recently?" stuttering more than I had on the first attempt.

"Oh, no I've been pretty busy at work since I've gotten back. What about you?"

"Actually, I have. I'm in a poetry workshop this semester, so I've been writing a lot."

Wow, that is a mouthful. I'll be impressed if she got any of that, I thought to myself.

"What?" I could hear her straining to try to put the words together.

As I repeated myself again, I felt every hope of appearing debonair vanish with my imaginings of what I assumed was going through her mind.

"A poetry workshop, I bet that's fun. I'm a part of a writer's group here, too, and I get a lot out of it."

"Cool. It's always helpful to have a group to bounce ideas off," I said feeling the energy of the conversation begin to relax.

"Yes, it is, and I've really enjoyed reading your poetry. Please keep sending more."

Yes, I'm in, I thought, as I beamed, "Of course I will. I'd love to read some more of your writing, also."

"Of course. I'd be happy to send you some more."

"Great!"

"I just got home, so I need to go, but it's been great talking to you!"

"Indeed it has," I said feeling my heart begin to pound once more, "Is it okay if I call you again?"

"I'd be delighted. I'll talk to you soon, then."

As we both signed off, I noticed that not only was every part of my body buzzing with electricity, but I was also aware that the nagging fears about being understood had totally subsided.

At the end of that night and still reeling from our conversation, I fell asleep, with a smile in my heart, only to find myself walking beside her in my dreams.

Four months later, when our email dialogue and phone conversations had developed into multiple daily occurrences, I found myself in a conversation with one of my friends.

"Who is it that you talk to all the time? Every time I see you, you're on the damn phone."

"Um, she's … my girlfriend. She lives in Alabama." Girlfriend, I thought to myself. What did I just say? Oh, she's going to love this one. I'll probably never talk to her again after I tell this to her.

I really had no intention of defining our relationship in any way at that point, particularly because I was almost certain that she had no designs beyond friendship. I was also not in the mood for another anti-climatic "let's just be friends," but something from within made me snicker at the thought of telling her about my conversation.

As I was walking away from my friend to return to campus, I felt an amazing concoction of excitement and nerves. I glanced at my watch; it was around 5 pm, and I was sure by now that Megan would be relaxing at her computer after dinner. It was a perfect time to call.

She answered and with a Cheshire grin that she swears now was visible through the phone lines. I giggled, "So I was talking with a friend today, and I referred to you as my girlfriend." A pause. A gulp. "Is that okay?"

"Yes, it's okay," she squeaked with the same amount of giddiness that had permeated my body and soul.

The funny thing was, it felt so natural to the both of us that, after hearing her initial response, our conversation immediately returned to its normal fare.

Several days later, I was contemplating her rapidly approaching birthday trying to figure out what gift could adequately represent what was unfolding before us. One afternoon, I took a stroll down to Fourth Avenue, a part of town where the storefronts are flavored with the hint of a Mexican Mercado and the sidewalks are lined with vendors peddling Tibetan knickknacks and an astonishing array of incense.

I popped into one store that housed a host of Navajo jewelry, and I found myself drawn to a plain silver cross with a small turquoise stone in the center. I closed my eyes, and the image of Megan's face and neck flashed before my eyes, wearing the piece on a thin silver chain. I bought the cross and moved on, feeling as though no piece of jewelry alone could encompass what was growing between us.

A few doors down, I stumbled into a fabric store that felt as warm and soft as all of the woven rugs and blankets stacked to the brim and draped over kiva ladders. I was immediately drawn to a light blue and white blanket and, upon picking it up, thought that it perfectly resembled the interweaving threads that bind relationships together within Native American tradition. While at the store, I also picked up a piece of leather thong, which I could use to wrap the blanket and attach the cross.

On my way home, a memory stirred in the back of my mind. I was at a training seminar where we were building a sweat lodge. It was early November, high in the mountains south of Tucson. I huddled near the fire in a futile attempt to stay warm. A friend of mine asked if I was cold.

I said, "No," but after several minutes he came to me and insisted that I take his blanket.

As I did so, he laughingly said, "Now Barton, I'm not marrying you just because I gave you my blanket."

I looked at him confused. He explained that in the Apache tradition, wrapping one's blanket about someone's shoulders represented betrothal between the two people.

Holding the blue and white blanket in my lap, I was semi-conscious of what the blanket symbolized. From the training that Megan and I shared, I was hopeful too, that she would recognize what my gift represented.

I raced home, folded the blanket neatly, took the leather cord and tied it around the blanket in the shape of a cross. Into the knot, I bound the piece of jewelry and then slipped in a poem addressed to My Love.

Dearest Megan,
Together we sing like angels before the Father
as our souls weave into His.
Melting bodies upon heaven's threshold,
we spark like lightening against the solitude of night.
The silken glow of your caress
ripples through my being like the
sun's gleam rousing the ocean's surface.
Here, we slip into the horizon, swimming as one.
Happy Birthday my love,
B

~ S. Barton Cutter, August 2003

Chapter Two

Poetry and Rose Petals

Twinkling Moons
When you smile at me,
your eyes twinkle
sparkling moons,
your arms wrap around me
inside
the blue and white blanket
we share.

-S. Barton Cutter, May 2003

As I walked into the bridal shop, the electric buzz of excitement was contagious. The chatter of my mom and to be mother-in-law as they flipped through wedding gowns hanging on the racks hummed in the background of white fabric and lace that draped over me. One after another, until I looked in the mirror and knew this was the perfect wedding gown. I was a princess, as all brides should be.

With veil in place, I walk down the makeshift aisle in front of a tri-fold mirror, and out of the corner of my eye, I caught my mother turning her head away so I wouldn't see her cry.

One year later, I stood in my mother's room for hours, the closet door open, looking at the white-laced wedding dress and veil folded perfectly on its hanger. Unworn. Memories echoed through the empty house, of voices long stilled.

Vague senses of the child-like excitement of walking into the bridal shop with my mother and mother-in-law to be still buzzed through my skin. The impression of my mother crying haunted me long after the posed prince, unmasked for who he really was, had taken off with an-other bride and my mother's breath had unexpectedly stilled in the night.

As I stood unmoving with the past haunting me, I couldn't find the right answer—should I move the dress from its place? In time it would be moved, cleaned and preserved. I would shove the awkward rectangular box into the dusty garage trying so hard to forget.

I had never expected to fall in love again.

Two years would pass, time filled with the logistical ordeals that come with death, an emptiness and fear that wrenched my body. I needed to get out of the house where I felt stifled by the hours spent going through my mother's overflowing wardrobe, sorting collections of knickknacks and a minefield of reminders that would inevitably throw me into an emotional breakdown.

I knew there was more to life; I just didn't know how to reach for the possibilities that seemed so far away.

My good friends Judy and Larry invited me to train with them in budo taijutsu. At the time, I didn't pay attention to the fact that it was a martial art, I simply trusted them when they assured me it would be good for my state of mind. I also knew that I had to get out of the house, and one night after work I found myself driving to the University of Alabama Quad.

My first thought was, what are they doing rolling around on the ground, and what am I doing here? At the time, I couldn't possibly comprehend how I could do any of this.

I watched my friends as they rolled, punching and kicking—dynamic and alive. Joining in, I felt silly and awkward at the way my body moved. Soon, though, I would be rolling, punching and kicking as the sky turned to dusk.

After only a few weeks, I decided to add a creative writing class, stepping back into the powerful flow of words, which once poured out through notebook after notebook. Unsure if this particular writing class was what I was looking for, I called the instructor.

"Hello, this is Jack," the voice said on the other end of the phone, which was oddly familiar.

"I'm Megan, and I'm interested in taking your writing class. Can you tell me a little more about it?"

"Megan, are you Megan who just started training?"

The question took my by surprise, and I paused a minute before answering. "Oh, yes, yes, it's me." Jack was a black belt in the same martial arts class. "Oh, yes, of course. I'll sign up for writing."

I was excited to return to the stream of consciousness prompt writing that filled my journals when I was younger. Along with the martial arts, journaling became a safe place for me to work through the sorrow that had become such a prominent fixture.

Nearly two and a half years later, I met several friends that I trained with out in Tucson, Arizona over Valentine's Day Weekend for an informal seminar. The warm winter days were spent in conversation and casual practice.

Being out west was stunning, not only the desert mountains and sun setting on red rocks but how I felt so free and connected in this space. The first time I went to Sedona was exactly one year after my mother's passing; I remember my mother had always talked about visiting Arizona and New Mexico.

Now, I was out here in this space, feeling so connected to the maternal earth. I was both excited and a bit anxious. What on earth was I doing out here, so far from what I knew? After mom's death, I didn't know what to do with myself other than going through the motions of the day. *What was I going to do now*, was a phrase that echoed across the first steps without her. The landscape settled the nervousness in my soul. I was quiet and at peace.

I was in the hallway of our friend's house, when Barton arrived, and all at once, there was this buzz, "Barton was here."

"Who was Barton," I wondered.

When I noticed the man in a wheelchair, I quietly questioned his ability, "How does he train in a wheelchair? Poor thing."

My thoughts quickly dissipated as we were introduced, and there was something vaguely familiar; I just couldn't put my finger on it. I gently held his tight-fisted hand, feeling bad somehow that he was in a wheelchair.

As soon as we said hello, he was off, and my attention turned towards other activities.

Several months later, I would return to the heat of Arizona for a longer workshop where my friends from Tucson and I served behind the scenes. As soon as I arrived, I was put to work in the kitchen cleaning dishes and preparing meals. Barton was also assigned to help in the kitchen and parked himself beside me.

With a towel in hand, Barton asked to help, too.

I didn't know what to do, so I stood over him, talking to him in my slow sweet Southern Alabama voice.

"No, I got it. Thanks, though."

After a few moments, an instructor who had been watching us took me by the arm and pulled me outside. "Do you have a problem with Barton?"

I shook my head. I didn't think so. She continued, "Look, he's been through training, he can handle it. He's a man, so don't patronize him."

Had I been patronizing him? I nodded and in my mind reviewed my words and tone. After that moment of being called out, I saw Barton's eyes radiate like the sun's rays through the kitchen window, surely brighter than my own.

Later in the day, we found ourselves together again tasked with cleaning an outside walkway. I slipped the broom handle into Barton's fingers, and he gripped tightly, proceeding to hit himself in the head with the end of the handle, laughing hysterically. I didn't need to ask if he was okay. I just smiled instead.

Barton asked, "Where do you work?"

Unable to pick up his speech pattern at first, it took several times of my asking him to repeat his question before I finally understood.

"I organize about fifty trade shows a year. I take care of everything from the booth itself, to logistics and publicity. What about you?"

Barton looked up, "I'm a student at the University of Arizona."

"What are you majoring in?"

"Creative writing." As Barton banged the broom around his wheelchair, I noticed the small short strokes he used collected a pile of dust and leaves.

I perked up, "Really? I majored in Creative Writing, too. What do you write?"

Barton continued sweeping, "Poetry."

I swept a pile of leaves off to the side. "Me, too. Poetry and short stories. I used to write a lot of poetry, but not as much anymore."

Barton beamed, "I'd love to read a few of your poems sometime. Before we leave, we need to swap email addresses or phone numbers."

"Sure, and I'd love to read some of your writing, too."

That evening, I walked out to the fire pit to tend the fire. With a blanket wrapped around my shoulders, the heat of the fire warmed the front of my body. Barton was at the far end of the campfire. The silver metal of his wheelchair sparkled from the reflection of flickering flames. In the light of the fire, Barton's eyes lit up. If there were other people around the fire, I didn't notice them. Everything around us melted into the background.

As Barton and I looked at each other across the flames, a wave of emotions began to rise within me. I could feel our connection growing, and I felt myself approaching an interior space where I would be called to embrace new choices. It was like we had known each other for a long time. I flirted with the attraction that percolated from a long forgotten place, but my mind couldn't comprehend being drawn to him.

The rest of the week, Barton and I hardly saw each other; we were so busy with the work that had to be done around the campgrounds. When the seminar was over, instructors and students alike took to packing and cleaning. I was walking across a wooden bridge when Sarah, a friend who was also working behind the scenes at the seminar ran up the path.

"Megan, Barton's leaving. He's been looking for you. You better hurry."

"Where is he?"

I followed her to the car already idling in the parking lot. Without any hesitation, I jumped in the backseat across Barton's lap. I pulled out a piece of paper from my pocket, tore off a small piece and scribbled my name, phone number and email. Tucking a small turquoise stone in the middle of the paper, I slipped it in his pocket with a quick kiss on the cheek. Before we could say anything else, he was off. Even then, after the rush of just a few minutes, I was slow to catch onto the connection growing between us.

Arriving home at midnight, I was blurry-eyed from the long journey. I dropped my bags on the floor, and I turned on my computer to check email since I was away for an entire week.

> Megan,
>
> I hope you got back home okay. I really enjoyed talking with you. Maybe we could swap poems sometime. Hope you have a great day.
>
> Barton

A smile splashed across my face. I really didn't think he would email me back, and I certainly wasn't expecting any contact from him as soon as I arrived home! I was exhausted, but the excitement of seeing his note gave me an adrenaline rush. I hadn't even unpacked, but I had to respond.

> Barton,
>
> You don't waste any time, do you? I would love to read some of your poetry, do send me some. Here's a story I just finished for my writing class and a few poems as well.
>
> Megan

My bed never felt so comfortable, and I drifted off to sleep with a new sense of curiosity and warmth rising in my soul. I dragged myself through the next day at work, swamped from several projects that needed immediate attention. It was then that I regretted being away from work. Though my co-workers were catching me up to date on all the projects I needed to attend to, my thoughts were preoccupied.

When I arrived home that evening, all I wanted to do was crawl back into bed. However, I just couldn't resist the urge to turn on my computer. Sure enough, Barton had written me back.

Megan,

Of course not, there's no time to waste!

I really enjoyed the stories and poem. You have a lot of nice subtlety that adds good depth without overwhelming the reader. By your description of how you write, it sounds like you are a true connoisseur of words. That is quite a gift, which many are lacking today. I agree that this writing exchange is wonderful and would also love to continue. Here are a few more blurbs for your perusal. Enjoy!

Love, B

Barton attached three poems; I printed them out and read them over and over before I fell asleep. This exchange of poetry and stories materialized everyday. I would wake up with a poem in my inbox. I would zip off a quick email before going to work, and print the poem he had written me so I could read it during my mid-morning break. By the time I went to bed, there was another poem to savor as I drifted off to sleep.

"He's just a friend," I would say when asked about the notes I had printed out to re-read over my lunch hour, but I didn't really talk about Barton or our connection. I had been through such a public display of losses in my life from the time after a broken engagement and my mother's death. Clearly, my mind had not caught up to my heart.

While I had come out of that period of mourning, I didn't believe that I could find love again. I didn't even know what the next step of my life would be. I still didn't recognize the love flourishing between emails. Our dance of words lasted several months, as I continued telling others, and myself, he was just a friend.

Until the flowers, that is. By August, Barton and I had swapped an entire volume of poetry and short stories. We made comments, suggestions, encouraged each other to write more and to revise more.

A few weeks before my birthday, I received a voicemail on a Saturday afternoon about some flowers that were supposed to be delivered. Apparently, the flower shop had left a door tag at my house, but I didn't remember seeing any sort of notice. The store had just closed, so it would be Monday before I could contact them to pick up the flowers.

Driving to the grocery store that evening, I kept thinking: *Who sent me flowers? It's not my birthday yet. Wait a minute. Barton - I bet Barton sent me flowers.*

On the phone that night, I could tell he was waiting for me to say something, but I didn't know why. On Monday morning, a vase of purple, pink and yellow flowers were delivered to my work.

> Together, we waltz at the cusp of creation.
> With all my love, B.

Arriving home, I set the vase of flowers on my desk and giggled to myself re-reading the poem. Moving as though I was on automatic pilot, I found myself in the garage, retrieving the white rectangular box, dusting it off, and moved it into my closet.

I couldn't deny the love in front of my face, which sparkled through those bright blue eyes, written in poems and electrified by the touch of our hands.

For my birthday, a package arrived in the mail, a box wrapped in brown paper; I knew it was from Barton. When I opened the box, a Native American blue and white blanket lay inside with a leather cord wrapped around it. A turquoise necklace was attached to the leather with a love poem tucked underneath. I unfolded the blanket and wrapped it around my shoulders.

The next time I traveled to Arizona in early November, we slept under my birthday gift, trusting that it would always keep us warm.

Moon Scenes

1.

Fantasy

At a glance, I caught the faint hue of moonlight
reflecting a castillian skyline across your abdomen.
When I shaved last,
you mentioned a clean taste. Now
stubble pricks like fresh espresso grounds
as I kiss lower.
Sighs whisper a supple siren in my ear.
The ocean is lapping at your thigh–
an energetic puppy begging, mixing salt and sex
between your toes. You and I lay as petals
pressed perfect into a mind
beached like fumbling starfish.

~ S. Barton Cutter, November 2004

Chapter Three

Mini Skirts and Go-Go Boots

Each breath with you is to truly
Know the beauty of the divine.
I love you, my wife to be.

·S. Barton Cutter, May 2003

I had planned to fly out to Tucson for Thanksgiving, but then Barton's mentor called to let me know there would be a ceremony where Barton would walk for the first time. I knew he had been working on standing and taking steps on his own. While I wasn't planning two trips to Arizona so close together, I couldn't miss it!

Two weeks before Thanksgiving, Barton and I saw each other for the first time since the martial arts seminar in May. Since the only flight I could find landed in Phoenix, I drove the hour to Tucson at midnight. Barton was waiting for me outside as I pulled into the parking lot. He met me at the car door. I moved over to his lap, and we kissed as a motorcycle pulled into the next parking space. I wasn't expecting for us to get into bed quite so quickly, but we were caught in the romance of the last six months, the poetry that dripped off our emails and the flowers that provided the aromatherapy of love.

Eventually we managed to get out of bed, and Barton took me on a tour of The University of Arizona. I sat in his lap and drove his motorized wheelchair, erratically all over campus. I squealed as we jerked to the edge of the sidewalk. Barton corrected the wheelchair, getting us back on track. I could hear him exhaling as he showed me how to push the joystick to avoid the hazards in front of us. Bystanders gawked as I laughed out loud as we made our way through campus. Two white doves soared just over our heads, and we could feel their wings move the air.

Barton took me to a restaurant where he claimed they had the best pizza in town; he was right. As I picked up a piece of cheesy pizza and put it gently in his mouth, we looked into each other's eyes. I could see the entire universe. We couldn't stop looking at each other; we also couldn't stop smiling. I found out that Barton couldn't smile and eat at the same time; it was a long lunch, interrupted only by one of his friends passing by. We polished off every bite of the pizza and made our way back to his apartment. Any fears I had about being intimate with Barton dissipated with the ecstasy that followed.

Later, our friends would call us Marianne and Gilligan on a "three-hour tour" since our absence at the seminar was apparent. However, I was unaware that there was even a martial arts seminar, and since Barton wanted to spend the day playing, I was surprised when I heard there were other things going on.

That night, we were the first ones at the park. I sat in Barton's lap, and he rubbed his hand along my fingers. "There's something missing."

"What?" I asked, but I knew already.

"I don't know; it seems as if your left hand is a bit bare. Someday soon I'll have to fix that."

I didn't respond. I just beamed as I lay my head on his chest.

Not too long after, our friends began to gather at a basketball court in the middle of the park. Barton was whisked away to talk with his mentor April. While Barton was preparing for the ceremony, I made small talk with those who I had not seen in a long time.

The ceremony signified the end of an apprenticeship training in the healing arts, based primarily on the Native American traditions of the southwest.

It wasn't until much later that I found out how he had not stood or walked before, and certainly not in front of family.

I knew Barton had been working on standing. I would call him months before, and he would be standing in a corner, huffing and puffing as I tried to understand him in between his breaths. I also heard about his working with Betsy, doing squats and stretches during the week and standing between park benches on the weekends.

When the ceremony began, Barton's mentor stood five to ten yards away; Barton stood up. Betsy had put a rectangle trashcan horizontally between Barton's knees, with weight inside, to help him keep his legs from crossing.

I watched on the sidelines and held my breath as he took one concentrated step after another, without assistance, to greet his mentor. As our friends came up one by one to bless him, tears streamed down my face, and I knew this was the man I was going to marry.

When someone asks me how Barton proposed, a smile expands across my face, "Well, which version do you want? There's the kosher version, the PG Rated version, and only a chosen few know everything. Let's just say, it's an engagement I'll never forget."

The two weeks between trips seemed like a lifetime, and I couldn't wait for Thanksgiving to arrive. Barton and I talked on the phone every night and dreamed of each other as we slept.

A few months earlier, my friend and co-worker Cindy had taken me shopping for an outfit to wear on a special occasion. It's rare that I wear short skirts, so when I came out of the dressing room with a black mini skirt and hot pink jacket, Cindy gasped. She added a pair of black go-go boots to complete the look.

Arriving at work early that day, she also straightened and styled my hair, dabbled blush on my face, and stroked eye shadow across my eyelids. I assured Cindy that if perhaps there were any surprises during the trip, I'd give her a call. I left just before lunch to drive to the airport.

Later, sitting on the plane, I giggled at the shock I gave my co-workers. Closing my eyes to take a nap, I became excited and suspicious that there may be a ring; after all, Barton had asked me for my ring size. However, I thought the timing would be around New Years, when he was scheduled to come visit me.

My flight didn't arrive until late Wednesday night. Walking out of the gate, I saw Barton's eyes widen and his smile spread across his face as he recognized me.

When we got to Barton's apartment, lit candles adorned every room. We could hardly get our clothes off fast enough.

Well after midnight, we were lying on the living room floor, my head resting on Barton's chest. Around three in the morning, we were still awake and talking. Out of nowhere, I felt Barton laughing, his chest moving up and down. I lifted my head up to feel his warm breath coming from the uninhibited smile on his face.

"What?"

He choked on his words between laughs and asked me to go find *The Norton Anthology of Poetry* on his bookshelf. In the buff, I quickly raced to Barton's bedroom. My vision was blurry from the candles flickering in his bedroom, so I struggled to find the book. Finally, I pulled it off the shelf and came back, poetry book in hand. When Barton saw the thick book of poetry, the giggles were uncontrollable.

"What?" I knew I had missed the joke but not understanding exactly what I had missed. Barton's laughter echoed throughout the apartment. Finally he took a breath and asked me, "Go back and look on the shelf again."

I had to go back into his bedroom to retrieve the little black box hidden on the bookshelf, now exposed without the book to disguise its presence.

"Oh my God!" burst through my lips over and over again.

"Will you marry me?"

"Are you serious? Oh my God."

"Will you marry me?"

"Yes." Barton was still on the floor laughing hysterically, and I threw my arms over him, nestling back under the blanket. I opened the box and slipped the white gold band with diamond in the middle onto my finger. It fit, perfectly.

I couldn't stop looking at my hands, and "Oh my God" became a mantra I would whisper with each breath over the next hour.

We began to fall asleep on the living room floor, but eventually moved back to Barton's bedroom, leaving just a few candles lit. Though we had only a few hours of sleep, Barton's assistant came in at 7 am to get him up. While Barton was getting dressed, I took a shower, staring at the ring on my finger. When Barton's assistant left, we couldn't help but climb back into bed for a few more hours of sleep.

By mid-afternoon, we knew we had to get up. After all, it was Thanksgiving and we had been invited to dinner at Betsy's house. When we arrived, I couldn't help but show my new engagement ring to Betsy.

The news of our engagement spread around the Thanksgiving table, and I showed off the ring. I couldn't stop looking at the simple band and the diamond sparkling between two gold posts. I was thankful for the man sitting next to me and all the possibilities that lay ahead of us.

That evening, I sat on Barton's lap in the parking deck overlooking the desert mountains, one of best views for the Tucson sunset. We were in love, starting our lives together, and that was all that mattered.

I was only going to look. My next-door neighbor Sarah said she knew of a good jeweler nearby, and she offered to drive me out there one afternoon. It was mid-September but even the three days between the time that Sarah mentioned the jeweler and when we planned to go seemed inexhaustible.

Rolling off the bus near the front of my apartment complex, I couldn't drive my chair fast enough. My chair flew down the steep hill to where I found Sarah knocking on my door to see if I was ready. We quickly exchanged my electric wheelchair for my lighter, more portable manual chair and headed to the car.

Getting in the car, I was excited by the prospect of what I might find; could this be the first step toward spending my life with Megan? The thought of this question brought me so much joy that when I stood to transfer into the car, I straightened my spine prematurely sending my wheelchair tipping backward with me still in it. Once my chair was back on all four wheels, I found my balance. Sarah helped me transfer into the front seat and we were off.

The store was only a couple miles up the road, but in that time, Sarah tried to tame my excitement. She tried to reason with me, reminding me that I had only spent a week with Megan and asked, "How could you possibly know that she is the one?"

But I did. The hours spent enraptured by Megan's soft voice on the phone coupled with our endless encounters during dreamtime made the innumerable images come to life so palpably through the verses I wrote her, that there was no way I could have been mistaken.

Megan was the one I was going to marry. By some divine providence, I found myself releasing all that I had once held in expectation of a bleak and lonely future.

When we arrived at the store, I was overtaken by excitement, and all of my willpower to merely browse collapsed. I knew there was no way I was coming home empty-handed. I looked at several rings and several diamonds, many of which were gaudy. Even the ones within my price range did not have the right feel to them.

After an hour or so of looking at each ring several times, Sarah sensed my rapidly deflating hopes. "We can look at some other places if you want, and we both know you don't have to buy anything today. It's not like you're proposing tomorrow."

"Perhaps you're right. Let me take one more look, and then we'll call it a day." I took one last glance at the display and realized I had overlooked a small white gold band with an equally small diamond set between two gold posts near the back of the counter.

I knew immediately this was the one, though I did not understand why. It was only after the fact that I came to recognize the symbolism of the gold posts as our individual connections to God and the diamond itself as our souls combining to make an integrated whole.

Overtaken by excitement, all four of my limbs began flailing in opposite directions as my hips and torso went into full extension. I let out a scream that this ring was the one I wanted, and my manual wheelchair began to careen backwards once again unable to contain the wildness of my body. I think the store clerk was taken aback by my display of enthusiasm. I bought the ring, my mission complete.

The whole way home from the jewelry store, the smile on my face was unrelenting. We filed out of the car at our apartment complex as Sarah's roommate was arriving home. All I wanted to do was call Megan, yet I knew there was no possible way to speak to her at that moment without exposing my excitement. I could only share my giddiness with Sarah and her roommate.

When the roommate heard all that transpired, her response was, "I thought you were only going to look. What happened?"

I beamed, "I can't explain it. The ring felt right to me. I had no choice; it was there."

They both laughed and shook their heads. For the past four months they had listened to me go on about how amazing Megan was and how we constantly dreamed of being together. They knew, as did Neal, my roommate, that I was merely biding my time until I had the opportunity to propose. They listened to me ramble for a good half an hour about Megan and my love for her. We went back to my apartment, and they helped me find a suitable hiding place for the ring.

After trying several places around my apartment where it could have easily been found by one of my direct support staff, I finally found the perfect place behind one of my favorite books, *The Norton Anthology of Modern Poetry.* It seemed appropriate to me, as it was words such as these that had made our love so strong.

When I talked to Megan later on the phone, it took everything I had not to show my excitement. After all, we had only been together as a couple for a little over a month. She only discovered how much I loved her at her birthday in August. Now it was mid-September and I already had an engagement ring.

The key now was to make sure that the size was correct without giving myself away. This was nearly impossible, as the only way I could find out her ring size was to ask. Trying not to raise her suspicions, I probed each moment of our conversations to casually inquire. Now, I am quite sure that any attempt at being sly was nothing more than a figment of my imagination.

She sent the ring size to me in an email. Fortunately, it was a perfect match with the ring I had bought. Over the next month, my excitement grew and, with each opportunity I had to show my closest friends the ring, I would erupt in laughter.

Three weeks before Thanksgiving, my dad and stepmother came to visit. There was much I wanted to share with them.

"Dad, Nancy, I've been working on something that you may not believe." I unfastened my seatbelt and planted my feet on the floor. "Dad, would you spot me?"

"Sure, what do you need?"

"Just put your arm out in front of me for a moment." Lightly grasping his hand, I came forward to center my weight over the balls of my feet, and delicately stood without any additional support.

Nancy exclaimed with a smile, "That's amazing."

"Thanks. That's not all." I said, still standing. "I've also been working on walking."

I sat back down in my chair. "Wow, that's really impressive," chuckled my dad with a reserved excitement.

"Well, there's a reason I'm doing all this. You remember Megan, the woman from Alabama that I've been telling you about?"

"Yes," they both gulp and nod. They only knew of Megan as an acquaintance.

"She's the one I'm going to ask to marry me. I'm not sure when, but I know it's coming, and I want to be able to walk her down the aisle."

"That's nice," stuttered my dad in surprise, "Are you sure marriage is the right avenue?"

"I am indeed."

Nancy chimed in, "I'm happy to hear you're in love, but if you get married, you could lose your benefits. Are you sure you'll be able to manage?"

"We'll find a way. At the moment, Megan does marketing for a firm in Alabama. I can get on her health insurance once we're married, unless I find a job first. In which case, we'll both be doubly covered. I know we can make it work."

Shifting her demeanor, Nancy smiled, "I'm glad you're so happy. It's wonderful to see."

Over the following week, my excitement to propose only increased. I constantly plotted my proposal. My plan at the time was to wait until New Year's, when I would be out with Megan in her home, but my excitement got the better of me.

Before I picked Megan up from the airport for Thanksgiving, Sarah and I spent an hour placing candles throughout my apartment, lighting them before leaving.

I did not expect to propose that night, but in the wee hours of the morning, lying in each other's arms, my excitement exploded into laughter, and I could not contain my joy. She asked what was so funny, and I tried to play it off as if it were nothing. She would not hear any of it, so I finally asked her to go find *The Norton's Anthology of Modern Poetry* from my bedroom.

When she came back with the book, it only increased my laughter and excitement. I couldn't believe I had to send her back for the ring. How could she have possibly missed it? I knew it was there. I had checked on it about once a week by showing it to friends, and I watched carefully as they put it back every time. I had total confidence that it was still resting safely where I had put it for the last two months.

When she finally found the box, all I heard from the bedroom was squealing. She kept repeating, "Oh my God, oh my God, oh my God, oh my God."

When she returned to where I was lying in the living room, I proposed. It was a miraculous yes.

Droplets fall as snow melts,
as sun glistens on pine bark.
Radiant light
fills the crisp air,
the mist of our breath
mingles
and rises.

~ Megan M. Cutter, February 13, 2007

Chapter Four

Kick Ass Wheels

A month after I proposed, Megan was completing a significant milestone in her training, which was to be marked with a small ceremony near the house of her mentor, Virginia. This also coincided with a martial arts seminar allowing us the opportunity to train together for the first time.

When I arrived in Washington DC, I picked up my bag and soon discovered that Megan's plane had been delayed. I sat patiently in baggage claim waiting for her. For some reason, flying alone had never presented me with any issues.

After an hour or so waiting, I was pleased to see my beauty racing down the corridor to greet me. Megan collected her bag and we located our rental car. Soon, we were driving through the snowy Maryland streets to Virginia's house, where we were staying.

Despite Megan's hesitancy driving in such icy conditions, we arrived expeditiously, even after passing their driveway three times only to find that Virginia and her husband Alan had not yet returned home from an evening out. We huddled in the car with only the warmth of our bodies to ward off the outside bitterness.

We stayed quite comfortable, and our friends arrived forty-five minutes later to sweaty undergarments hanging from the rearview mirror.

Alan came to the passenger's side door, tapping on the foggy windows while trying to keep a straight face. "You okay in there?"

Megan cracked the window, "Yea, we're good. How about you?" I smiled.

"Great, let's get you guys inside."

Megan scurried to get our clothes semi-organized as Alan opened the door to carry me in.

The next morning, after the requisite amount of teasing by our friends over breakfast, we were off to the martial arts seminar. One of the unique aspects about budo taijutsu is that, in order to get the most learning out of a given exercise, the attacker needs to have a committed intent. Not that we move fast. In fact, we move at a relatively slow speed while training. However, if one's intent isn't realistic, the other person is not able to do the technique, never mind learning anything about how to do it.

In training, I rely on people to give me realistic attacks so that I can then use their momentum and intent to manipulate their balance and protect myself. All too often, however, people see my wheelchair, assume I am incapable of training, and do not commit while working with me. The result is often a lack of connection in the space where a dynamic relationship ought to grow.

Here is where I have a unique opportunity to help them learn, not only how to be a better attacker within the martial arts, but also how to bring greater vitality into their day-to-day relationships.

I usually allow the attacker to punch in this non-committal manner before mentioning the lack of energy between us. I then ask why. New students often admit their unwillingness to commit, pointing out the inability to focus their intent for fear of hurting me.

My response, "First of all, I'm a black belt, I can take care of myself. Secondly, if you pull your punches with me, is that empowering me to grow into a better human being or is it patronizing me to maintain the status quo and not improve?

If it's the latter, how does that serve humanity?"

This usually knocks them out of their complacency although it may take some more encouragement on my part to help them trust that both of us will survive and in fact grow through this process.

It's not everyday a couple becomes closer through training in the martial arts. I had been waiting for this opportunity to train with Megan for months simply because it had always been a fantasy of mine to fall in love with a woman who was just as eager to train as I was. At the same time, I also suspected she would feel even more uncomfortable than most attacking me for the first time.

She stood in front of me, our eyes connecting as we bowed to one another. I felt both of us fighting back the impulse to explode in laughter. We were trying to be serious, but it was impossible. I knew once she attacked, it would only be an opportunity for me to pull her into a warm embrace. My body smiled, but despite the possibility of holding her, I knew this was still time for us to train.

Megan stepped back, brought her fist up to the side of her cheek and prepared to punch. She stepped forward and extended her arm, fist loosely clinched, toward my forehead. As her fist neared my face, I sensed her timidity while her fist faltered from a lack of momentum three inches from my head.

"No, you have to hit me. I can't train unless it's a real punch. Now clean my clock."

Megan punched again. This time with more intent. Her fist met my forehead with full impact. I exclaimed, "That's better! Now we can play."

Megan stepped back, feeling more confident. As she did, her body fell into perfect alignment making even the most professional ballerina envious. Shifting her weight forward, the first two knuckles on her fist barreled without inhibition directly at my jaw.

At the last moment, I shifted my head to the side as the length of her forearm grazed the follicles on my cheek. I pivoted to face her arm and, with an open mouth, I bore my front teeth into her forearm. The weight of my head and torso, combined with her incoming momentum, overthrew the balance of my wheelchair. I toppled, chair and all, onto the inside of Megan's leg as we both fell to the mat.

"I can't believe you bit me!" Megan said in astonishment.

"Whatever works," I laughed as I ground my leg-rest further into her sciatic nerve.

I had always been intrigued by Eastern culture and drawn to the martial arts. Perhaps this was because I was born in Hong Kong, or perhaps, at some level, I recognized martial arts offered something I needed and could not find elsewhere. My parents tried for many years to find a teacher willing to take me on as a student. This search led to dead end after dead end.

Finally, in high school, I took part in the martial arts club held in the gym after school. I also recognized, however, that the modern version I was studying was limited in terms of what it would be able to offer me, both physically and intellectually.

When I left for college, I continued the search for a martial art that embraced physical aspects as well as philosophical and spiritual components. At the time, I was dabbling in meditation while practicing martial arts, and I began to recognize the combination was much more profound than I could fathom.

In the midst of my search, a dorm mate introduced me to a small group of martial artists who were training in budo taijutsu on the university quad. To say that I was intrigued would have been an understatement, and I began immediately loving every minute.

Over the first several months, my teachers, one of whom had a disability himself, did a brilliant job of breaking down the movements and directing me to find greater intention in how my body moved and responded to certain stimuli. This, combined with an increasingly regular meditation practice on my own, began to open unexpected doors. I noticed that as my concentration increased, I was able to focus, relax, and move my body more smoothly, bypassing the spasticity to which I had grown accustomed.

I also observed myself less bothered by external activities that did not go according to my own expectations. Still, I was surprised at how much the relaxation was impacting me physically. Because of my Cerebral Palsy, I had believed there was not room for improvement.

I was reluctant to attribute all of my progress to my deepening practices of martial arts and meditation. While I know they played a role, I was also aware of other factors that may have also contributed to the marked improvement. Namely, a spasticity medication and moving to sunny and warm deserts of Tucson from the cold northern climate of Chicago.

Over time, I began to work more consistently with the one teacher, Sky, who also had a disability, and he eventually became a mentor and guide for me. Much of this was due to his ability to perceive how my body functioned and guide me to find appropriate adaptations. In many ways, his insights and support made him my first positive experience with someone else with a disability.

While I had met plenty of people with disabilities in the past, he was the first to show me what I had already believed in my heart: the disability itself does not matter. Rather, what matters is what we make of our experience, disability or not, that determines our ability to persevere.

In class, this perspective was always evident in Sky's teaching. For each technique Sky would begin by having two students perform the move standing. He would follow this by walking us through, step by step as the two students provided visual example of his words. Finally, he would then have someone attack him. At which point he did his version of the technique in his wheelchair.

During our conversations, Sky was always on the look out for the one seed of wisdom that would shift my perspective from what I told myself I couldn't do to a way in which I could see success.

In retrospect, I had no idea how far the growth I was experiencing might carry me. As we worked together in both martial arts and the practice of meditation, he guided me to see how the two intertwined and fortified one another, strengthening the capacities of both.

There came a time, after several years of training, when the benefits I was experiencing could not be written off as happenstance, and this drove me deeper to discover a profound connection to what I believed to be an energy pervading everything.

The longer I trained, however, the clearer and stronger my connection to God, or something larger than me, became.

Throughout high school and into freshman year of college, I denied the concept of a single higher power. Though I was open to the idea there was an energy that flows through our existence, I was reluctant to name it, and even more reluctant to acknowledge I was in relationship with it.

Integrating this realization into my daily life outside of training offered me the choice to let go of many beliefs, such as accepting what it meant to have a disability and the possibilities for my life as a man regardless of what limitations I faced.

Megan

Whenever I tell someone that Barton and I met training in martial arts, my words are met by a raised eyebrow.

"How can Barton train in martial arts?"

Until that first weekend we trained together, I had the same skepticism. Wheelchair, martial arts? An assumption of non-physicality in a practice that is perceived as being fully physical. Now, I give a clever smile, "You'll have to come out and watch."

There is no description to fit the movement of Barton's training. An ankle caught under foot pedals, metal pieces of the armrest or just the right pressure to send an attacker flailing over Barton's wheelchair.

I began practicing martial arts because I thought I needed something to do as I was recovering from a broken heart, but what I was really looking for was healing, to find these pieces inside of me that I had sacrificed for someone else. Even in my writing class with Jack, I was known as the angry white girl, writing my rage of the betrayal that I had felt across the page.

I began training in February of 2000, and for a while, I was still trying to hang onto a relationship that could not be salvaged.

I needed to come to a place where I could let go, and martial arts became an environment where I could let go of it all, and I was okay. Punching and kicking men, in a healthy environment, was a good release, and I was surprised to discover both physical and mental strength within me.

How ironic it was when I realized the men in my martial arts class were all good-hearted men who respected women. Instead of belittling or patronizing me, they were there to help me learn, and they respected what I had to offer. I found myself, not only with more confidence, but I also began to look at the qualities of a good man. Clearly it was not in the relationship I had been in, and I began to find the strength to stand on my own.

Not only that, but I was learning how to take care of my family as well. One spring weekend, my mother came with me to a seminar, and Jack taught her how to use her cane to protect herself. I was excited to be sharing what I was learning with those I loved.

When my mother passed away, I was unprepared for what was to come. Not only the emotional grief, but also the legal process, sorting through items and now, living on my own. Overnight, I had gone from the comfort of being a daughter living at home with my mom to a full-fledged adult dealing with the complications of everyday life. A day after dealing with a leaky roof, a blown car tire and an overheated oven, I collapsed on the floor, feeling the emotional weight bearing down on my shoulders.

Training in martial arts and creative journaling became tools to process my grief and take the first steps into a new and unfamiliar world. As I explored how my body worked with an opponent, I also learned how to navigate the chaos I was experiencing everyday. In class, the point was to keep moving, no matter what, and this was certainly true in the challenges after my mother's death.

While I began training by needing to expel aggression and heal from a broken heart, I found something more profound. I found what I was willing to give up in the relationship I had been in, and now returned to the love of writing as a way to express my voice.

Barton and I only trained a couple of times together before we were engaged. That spring, when he graduated from school in Tucson, I was overjoyed when Barton told me he was on his way to Tuscaloosa.

His father picked him up from school, and they drove across country to Alabama.

Not only did Barton have to adjust to a new community in a small southern town that was not accessible, but the cold humid winter was a far cry from the warm Tucson sun where Barton was used to training.

That first winter in Alabama, Barton would get so cold from training outside, he would shiver until he was sick. His skin was so frigid, I almost didn't know if there was blood moving. More than once we drove home, just to wrap Barton in as many blankets as we could find to get him warm.

Our friends who trained not only worked with us together as a team, but they gave Barton things to work on for individual exercises and standing. I watched as Barton would lie on the grass, his legs doing bicycle kicks or side stretches, sweat running down his face.

When we ordered the walker that Barton still uses to stand every morning, it arrived in a box. I spread all of the bolts, screws and pieces across the living room floor, desperately trying to understand the instructions only to have Barton throw half of the pieces out, creating his own walking contraption. This would become our classic first disagreement.

At the end of the day, Barton was beaming as he stood in the walker for the first time. I held the handlebars stable as the walker slightly tipped back and forth as he walked across the living room floor.

Standing and walking soon became just as critical as training in the same way that swimming or a morning walk with our dogs became essential for me.

Our relationship grew as we trained together. Megan and I found that as a couple, our studies of the art took on different meanings. As we both had trained in budo taijutsu, we realized a need to function as a cohesive unit, utilizing our individual strengths rather than operating as individuals. We began exploring the dynamics of defending ourselves as a couple.

When Megan and I were out in the community, I was often in my manual wheelchair due to a lack of accessibility. More than once, a stranger off the street would approach us to help Megan. Was this person a good-natured Samaritan or someone who wanted to take advantage of the situation? It became apparent to both of us that my limited mobility combined with our need to help me transfer in and out of a car, made us more vulnerable.

With this in mind, we began using class time to explore these scenarios of walking down the street, getting in and out of our car, and being approached by someone we didn't know.

We worked in tandem and found ways to minimize these vulnerabilities and learned how to move efficiently while staying safe.

As we trained with these dynamics, we found our communication between one another was much more subtle and streamlined and the way we navigated difficulties became more fluid. This subtlety and depth of connection expanded beyond the realm of training into our daily lives.

Once we moved to Raleigh, we continued to explore some of these dynamics, but to a lesser extent, as the focus of our training reverted to deepening our individual skills, believing that as we grew as individuals, we would then be able to work even more efficiently as a team. Such was the case as our ability to train together shifted, as did the way we decided to balance our training activities.

Megan

Some time after our move, I stopped training every week, to focus on new relationships and networks with our neighbors, writing community and within local organizations.

Not only that, but the dynamics of our relationship would change, and arriving home so late multiple times a week sent me into a cranky sleep-deprived attitude; one that was unpleasant for everyone.

Barton would find rides to training, and every so often he would come home with red scrapes along his elbow or chin.

"What did you do?"

"Fell out of my wheelchair."

"Ouch."

The Barton smile would extend across his face, "Multiple times."

"Okay." I would nod, somehow putting the pieces together that Barton had thrown himself out of his wheelchair multiple times, working on falling or rolling onto the floor.

There are nights when I drive Barton over to the dojo, and while he's training, I have a night off to write. We're conscious of our schedule, how training is so vital for Barton and how I need a break once in a while.

And, although I choose not to train in budo taijutsu at the moment, I look for the right time to return and support Barton's efforts in teaching self-defense seminars we've designed specifically for those of all abilities.

When I close my eyes
to sink into the night,
you lightly brush my hand.
Dipping into canyons,
we soar over rock and water,
ascending to the stars.
I move to your touch,
your heart,
a rhythm that moves the waves.
You sing me a lullaby,
rocking me in the treetops,
and we touch the moon.

As morning sun wakes,
we float on azure clouds,
like dew dripping from tree-tips.
We nestle like the morning doves
cooing, warming damp feathers
in the new day.
I wake from slumber,
not wanting to move
glistening in delight
as morning rays
warm my skin.

To my love,

Megan

Chapter Five

The Dances That Spun Our Families Around

Thanksgiving afternoon, we decided to call our parents to tell them of our engagement. I didn't think about the fact that I had not told my father anything about Barton other than that he was a writer who lived in Tucson.

For my birthday in August, I told my father, "There's this guy in Tucson, he's a writer and he trains in martial arts. We've become really good friends. I like him."

But I was too nervous to tell my father and stepmother about Barton having Cerebral Palsy and using a wheelchair to get around, or how close we had become in such a short amount of time for a long-distance relationship. I wasn't thinking at all about questions or explanations. I was too excited about the night before.

Dad answered the phone on Thanksgiving morning. I burst out, "Dad, I'm engaged!"

"To who?" he asked. All of our parents had the same reaction.

I told him and my stepmother about Barton, writing, training, everything I could, but I only received a cool "congratulations" on the phone. I didn't realize how unbelievable it all seemed.

As the days passed, I was too wrapped up in post-engagement bliss to notice my dad hadn't called me back since I had arrived in Alabama. Nearly a week later, I wondered if I should call him. I wondered, "Shouldn't he have called me back, especially since I was engaged? Was he mad? Disappointed? Angry at me?"

When I did call my father's house over the following weekend, my brother answered.

I cheerfully rambled, "Hey Scott, how are you? Did dad tell you? I'm engaged!"

My brother was shocked, and it became clear my father hadn't said a word to anybody.

When dad got on the phone, I asked, "Dad, why didn't you tell Scott?"

"Well, Megan, I didn't know what to say. I don't know anything about Barton. What would I tell family?"

I didn't have a response. Words that came out of my mouth were automatic, "I don't know. I'd love for you to meet Barton. We're training in December."

After we hung up, I was crestfallen, "He didn't tell anyone in our family. It's like I don't even exist."

Upon reflection, Barton and I agree, if we have a daughter who did this to us, Barton would run over the guys legs and maybe a few other parts as well.

Three weeks later, Megan invited her father to join us in Washington D.C. for a martial arts seminar we were both attending. This would be the first time I would meet him, and while I wish I could say I was bursting with excitement, the truth is I was trembling in trepidation.

During the afternoon training period, I noticed a man in a red shirt quietly enter the dojo and take a seat with some others who were observing. I knew immediately that this was Megan's father. His attempts at invisibility did not go far in a room full of ninja, and within seconds, Megan and several other friends of ours went over to greet him and soothe his apparent anxiety.

Prior to his arrival, my timing and focus in training was finding its rhythm and flow. But my own anxieties got the better of me the minute I saw him, and I received a punch in my face from my training partner. I thought, "Wow, I sure hope this isn't telling of the rest of our relationship."

Megan went over to greet him with a hug. They smiled briefly at each other and began to chat, Megan wringing her hands with nervousness. A minute later, Megan glanced over and pointed me out to her father; following the line of her finger, he caught my eye and nodded as they made their way over to me.

Megan broke the ice, "Dad, I'd like you to meet Barton. Barton, this is my father, Louis."

"Hello sir, it's great to meet you," I said with a hopeful grin.

"Hi Barton, it's a pleasure to meet you, too. Megan's told me much about you. It looks like you're having a good time training."

"Yes, it's been a good weekend. How was your flight up?"

After a hasty conversation with a couple of awkward pauses, Louis decided to sit down and watch as we returned to training.

That evening, we went to the hotel where Louis was staying so we could change our clothes and get ready for dinner. When we arrived at the hotel, Louis hopped out of the car quickly; Megan followed and began to pull my wheelchair out of the trunk. As she started to assemble my chair, I could feel Louis' tension begin to mount again as he paced the length of the car.

Once my chair was put together and Megan helped me out of the car, we headed into the hotel. Louis let Megan and me use his room to change out of our training clothes and into out dinner attire. Megan helped me change first. We were almost done when, picking up my tie, Megan shot me a perplexed look. "I have no idea how to tie a tie!"

"Fear not, my love. I brought directions. They are in the bag."

Megan rummaged a little further and pulled out a crumbled piece of paper with directions on the proper way to form a half Windsor knot. "What the hell is this?"

"It's directions. Here, look. Put the tie around me; make the fat end really long and the thin end pretty short."

I then talked Megan through the steps, and she, with an end of the tie in each hand, crisscrossed the ends of the tie back and forth in a manner akin to a circus clown in the midst of a juggling act gone awry. The resulting knot was amazingly clean, but the back end of the tie was somehow twice as long as the front end.

"What? That can't be right. Something's wrong."

"It's not that bad; you almost have it. Let's try again." We went through it again and on her second attempt, we corrected the length. Still, the knot itself looked like the tangled strings of a marionette. Trying to alleviate her growing frustration, I mentioned that she could ask her dad for help.

"Damn it, I'm going to get this." With her determination resolute, she made one more attempt, and I found myself wearing a beautifully done tie. After some finishing touches, Megan wheeled me out to the lobby where her dad had been waiting on us. Then Megan left us alone so she could return to the room and change.

There we were, face to face and alone for the first time. Here was my opportunity to establish a relationship with him, and more importantly, it was likely the only chance I would have to ask for Megan's hand and his blessing.

"Louis, I'm really glad that we're finally meeting. I know how important Megan is to you, and I love her so very much. I promise you that I will do all I can to provide for her and support her, and I would like to ask for your blessing." I paused with a gulp.

"I'm sure you are a good man, and I appreciate your wanting to ask me for my blessing. Megan's been through a lot in her previous relationship, and it's really important to me that I know whoever she's with well before I offer my blessing. I'm sure you understand."

"I can respect that. I hope we have the chance to get to know each other better over the coming months and years. I also hope you can respect our decision not to wait."

He nodded, and we paused in quiet understanding of one another. I heard Megan approaching from the hallway behind me.

Years later, we received a powerful and loving letter from Louis:

> Barton, I remember our first meeting and especially our conversation while waiting on Megan to get dressed. You asked my permission for you to marry Megan. When I said that you and Megan would have to make that decision and that I did not know you well enough to say much about it, you came right back with, "Well, I hope you will one day." Your question was very respectful and I appreciated that. I wanted my answer to be honest and respectful to you also. I still would say that you and Megan would have to make your decisions, hopefully with input from both of your families. I also want you to know directly what I hope you both experience with me that I do bless your marriage and life together. Barton, I do know you much better now and I think of you as a person of strength and integrity. Your resilience, forged through your journey through the valleys and mountaintops of your life, is an asset to your career as well as your marriage to Megan. You bring light to Megan's eyes and joy and laughter to her life, and for that, I am grateful!

Barton traveled to Alabama between Christmas and New Year's, and we spent a romantic week together. The weather was so warm, one afternoon we ventured out to the Quad at the University of Alabama, lay down a blanket and had a picnic as we read poetry to each other.

During the week, we drove to Birmingham where Barton's mom

would not only meet me for the first time, she would meet my father, stepmother and brother at the same time that my stepmother and brother would be meeting Barton. Clearly we had switched the traditional order of how meeting the parents is supposed to work.

The drive from Tuscaloosa to Birmingham was excruciating. I am sure that the drive from Atlanta to Birmingham was even longer for my father, stepmother, and brother. Barton's mother had been in Birmingham, unfortunately because of the deteriorating health of her own mother. I was so nervous that I fussed over directions to get to The Summit Mall, and became irritated over the lack of parking spaces once we arrived.

As we were getting out of the car, Barton's mom Catherine spotted us, and came over to give Barton a hug, then introduced herself to me as we exchanged a cordial hug. I also noticed how her clothing looked similar to the style my mother wore, eclectic and elegant.

The three of us walked to the door of the restaurant, when my dad, stepmother Linda and half brother Scott walked up the sidewalk to greet us as well. Scott had grown in height, and I thought about how he looked so similar to my grandfather who had passed away several years prior. We took a few minutes to give introductions to everyone before we sat down at a table.

Once we settled down at a table, there was clear tension, as no one knew exactly what to say after formal introductions. We all became busy figuring out what to order.

I filled in the silence by sharing the first time Barton and I went out to eat in Tucson, "We went to a Japanese restaurant, and I was using a fork with the rice. I got more rice on Barton than actually in his mouth. On the last bite, Barton smiled and said, 'Why don't you use a spoon?'"

Catherine was the only one who chuckled, "At least he didn't try to make you use chopsticks."

Scott also took the edge off by making jokes at the expense of our waitress, who continually mixed up our drink and food order.

After we laughed at the situation of switching plates, Barton's mother and my father began talking about growing up in Alabama, two different experiences, but it gave them a commonality the conversation could revolve around, instead of the inconvenient reality that the two of us were getting married to their dismay. Barton had hoped their experiences of living in Alabama would be the start of a close relationship between them.

I observed how quiet Linda, my stepmother was during the entire meal. I am sure she was just trying to take everything in, but I couldn't help but think about what she must think of me.

At the close of lunch, there was another commotion as we gathered to say good-byes. Both Barton and I were hopeful that there was a beginning of a friendship between families, but we were relieved to have this meeting behind us.

Instead of driving back to Tuscaloosa, Barton and I drove over to his grandmother's house in Birmingham where I would drop him off with his mother. I stayed for a little while, the nerves not subsiding at all, before driving home alone.

Since I was already in Birmingham, my aunt had scheduled a meeting with the president of a disability organization. I assumed this would be a great opportunity to see what kind of services this organization could provide. Since all of our parents had concerns for how we would manage, I was excited and hopeful to finally have someone on our side.

My aunt and I toured their facility and finally ended up sitting in the boardroom office around a table with swivel chairs. I listened to the president talk about how difficult it was for people with disabilities. Life would be hard. There would be few support services. How would we manage? He advised me that we should not get married. It would simply be too hard.

I sat in the chair, unable to respond. I was dumb-founded. This organization was supposed to support people with disabilities living full lives in the community. I thought they were supposed to advocate for them, to stand up and say, "Yes it is hard, but we can support you in living a life together."

I listened as issue after issue was brought to the table such as housing, transportation, employment, and direct care services, which were the primary ones.

I would be taking care of Barton, and it would be too much for me.

I had no answers. No response. I could only listen and absorb.

Riding home, I was furious. I remember speeding as I thought, "How dare he tell me it is too difficult to marry Barton. He doesn't even know Barton."

My head fell between my hands gripping the steering wheel at a stoplight. My family. My thoughts raced, "My father. Oh, God. I wonder how fast it's going to take my aunt to call my father and tell him verbatim that it was recommended that we not get married, that managing our lives would simply be too hard, only to reinforce my family's view of Barton, and the craziness of marrying someone who has a developmental disability."

Not long after, I was summoned to a meeting with my father and stepmother in Decatur, GA. We went out to breakfast at a local restaurant, and I fielded question after question about what it would be like living with Barton, marrying a man with a disability. Again, how would we manage? Would he be able to support me? How would we live? Would I be the sole caretaker?

My father advised us not to live together before we were married. Barton should move to Tuscaloosa, but find his own place to live. We should see if it works out and then get married. I understood this perspective, as we should take more time to deepen our relationship. I couldn't help but think how living apart would have been such a waste of money and resources for Barton. I had plenty of the space for the two of us in my mother's house. Moreover, Barton and I both knew it would not have been feasible for him to live successfully in a town that had no accessibility.

I wanted to be able to ease all of their fears, to assure them I was making the right decision for me, that I knew what I was doing. But there was no way I could address all of these issues in one meeting.

I could only be optimistic in my response, defiant and stubborn. "This is what we are doing. I love him. I'm sorry if it's not agreeable with you. This is what I want. We are getting married."

There was no resolution to the meeting. They had concerns. I didn't care; I was in love.

My grandmother was also visiting my dad's house for the Christmas holidays. One afternoon, my father said to me, "Your grandmother would love to spend some time with you. She was just waking from an afternoon nap. Why don't you go see her?"

I poked my head in the door, "Grandmother, are you awake?"

She was resting on her bed after a mid-day nap, and motioned for me to sit me down beside her.

She looked right at me and said, "I've worked with handicapped people, for many years, and I just don't see why you would marry someone who is retarded."

I thought, "Barton. Retarded? He's one of the smartest men I know."

Would she have listened if I had talked about how he had graduated from The University of Arizona in Creative Writing? That he was a black belt in martial arts? How he had already talked about how he could provide for me once we were married?

My grandmother went on about the difficulties of marriage. How I should marry a nice reputable young man, though unsaid, a doctor or lawyer like the rest of my cousins. It was true. I was always the black sheep on my father's side of the family. I was the artist, the writer, and in many ways my life was different from that of my cousins.

I ignored my grandmother and instead talked to her about how we met and what our plans were for our lives together. I chatted about Barton's humor and charm, how hard he worked to become independent, and his determination.

It wasn't enough. I was asked again to "think very hard" about my decision to marry Barton.

I did; it didn't change.

The spring after our engagement became this odd time of trying to connect our families so they could get to know one another. Distance provided a barrier that prevented us from making headway, and we began communicating in other ways.

Letter from my Father

March 2004

Megan,

It has taken me a while to write this to you. I began earlier this week but now cannot find it on my computer. That I have taken so long tells me that I have a lot of anxious energy bound up in this conversation with you. I have wanted to be as loving and as thoughtful about this as possible.

One thing that I got from our conversation about a week and a half ago was that you and Barton were concentrating on your relationship and how you feel about each other and you thought my concerns were of a very different nature—about how you both would manage the logistics of marriage and your life together. Did I get that right?

I remember a number of our conversations about life events in which I did go to the logistics first and missed how you were feeling and I do not want this to be that way. However, your concern makes sense to me because that is a typical way for me to approach an issue. I think both the feelings and the management of your life as a couple are important. I would imagine if we had spent more time with you and Barton and had shared your thoughts and feelings along the way that I would not have as many questions for you.

I am very interested in you and in how you are feeling about your relationship with Barton and your dreams for your relationship and the future. I do want to pay attention to those as well as to questions I might have about how you two have thought out how you will manage your life together.

I do want to know about the more logistical aspects of your marriage and relocation. You said that you were beginning to think that Birmingham and Alabama may not be the place for you to relocate. What other places are you considering? I do not know what the resources are like in Atlanta but may find out soon. I have a friend who has a 21-year-old daughter with Cerebral Palsy and am planning a lunch with her so that I can become more informed about the condition as well as implications for your life together as well as our life as a larger family after your marriage.

What would help me, given the quickness of your getting to a place in your relationship that you are ready to marry, is to know more about several areas of your planning your life together. I truly ask these from interest and concern. I do think the practical concerns of a married life together are important because they will be in place to support the two of you by giving you direction when things are good and by supporting you both together when the going is more difficult.

I am interested in how you two have planned to manage your lives financially. It seems to me that to be on a solid foundation you both would need to have jobs that can support you or a plan that makes good financial sense until you can relocate and find jobs or find jobs and relocate.

As you said to me several weeks ago, you should be able to get a job paying more than you are now making. A part of this plan might also be your knowing if Barton's family has made any provisions for him financially since you have said that you will need to get extra help to take care of him at least once a day. He may qualify for SSI but from my experience with that many years ago, it is not much at all. That also may not be available when he finds a job.

Given the special needs that Barton has for his mainte-
nance and care what kinds of support do you need and
what is available for him. I am guessing that you can do
some of the manual labor and lifting of him. However,
in addition to what you can do, what have you thought
you will need for him and what kind of resources are
there for you all for managing that?

I am also wondering what support the two of you have
thought you will need for yourselves as you live your
life together. You have told me that Barton gives to you
as you give to him and I can see that when I see the
two of you together.   However, when I think of the
many years of your life together it seems to me that
you will bear most of the doing and managing of the
household. I am certain you will work that out as you
live together but I am wondering if you have thought
of this as you plan your life together.

My hope has been to raise these issues so that I can
come to understand your thinking and planning as we
look forward to your marriage with Barton. My goal is
to be able to celebrate this special time with you.

I Love you,

Dad

My father's letter was warranted—there were questions and concerns
about how we would live together, but how could I possibly explain?
I was a young woman in love, and I knew what I wanted to do. In
many ways, I was still exerting my own independence.

I didn't have all the answers. I didn't have any. I did the best I could
to make them up. I knew Barton was working hard to find contacts
and had actually contacted disability organizations, not to find
services, but instead to pitch himself and to find work at these very
organizations. I didn't know how to appease my father, give him the
security he needed to believe we would be okay, stepping out into the
unknown without these services.

I did what any daughter or son would do—I gave him as much as I knew and made up the rest.

My response to my father was punchy and strong. This meek little girl I had been for so long was now ready to speak, but formulating and focusing these words was difficult as I was still struggling to find my own voice. Mixed within these words defending our relationship leaked emotion from after the death of my mother, a stubborn and defiant daughter, and attempting to define my beliefs of finding love.

Letter From a Daughter

March 2004

Dear Dad,

Thank you for your words of love and concern. I can see you are coming from a point of trying to understand why Barton & I would choose to get married. And I do feel like you want to come to place of joy and celebration when we get married. Barton & I are planning our lives together. I also agree there are practical decisions we will need to make and take into consideration to make our marriage successful. Yet, even if all that was there—the logical & practical decisions were taken care of—that would not sustain us because it is not the foundation of our relationship.

We have decided that we will not get the support we will need in Alabama, so we are looking at Raleigh-Durham, North Carolina. We will go there for Spring Break, as I believe I have spoken about to scout and research the area. Barton will be setting up appointments with United Cerebral Palsy in Raleigh to discuss the specific requirements for needs including his use of their employment assistance program, personal care and other assistance. Sometimes you have to live there 6 months before taking advantage of the program, so we will find out all the details in March.

His case worker is also assisting him, and she is working on getting his needs (insurance transferred, etc.) met in

AL for the time he is here and then working in NC, though we are planning to move as soon as one of us gets a job in North Carolina. Both of us are planning on working and finding jobs. There is a dojo, and we will continue training, teaching & learning.

In terms of personal care, Barton will have someone come in the morning & evening. In Tuscaloosa, we will piece this together, as there is no support for these resources. Tuscaloosa will be difficult because there is no busing system, so the faster we can get out, the better. In North Carolina, when we meet with United Cerebral Palsy, they may have some suggestions for this kind of care. We will put this into our budget and plan accordingly. Barton is working on standing, exercises and walking. It is profound how far he has come. I will be there to support him, but he will do the work on getting there.

We have discussed some of the financial details, and will get into more of the details as Barton moves here and we work those out. Barton does not have much parental support financially, as neither do I, and we will discuss these issues. Once we get settled, we will put together a portfolio for the future, yet it is important for us to get settled first.

You also have concern over my bearing and managing most of the household, and how much I will be a "caretaker." I understand your concern as from just the physical point of view; Barton does not look like he could take care of me. But our relationship is both spiritual and physical. Barton is a man, and he is planning on providing for me just like any other man. Daily living may be carried out differently, that does not mean it is any less valid or important. You talk about it like Barton is a burden I must bear. I see our relationship and our lives together as a gift that I am privileged and honored to have found.

After mom died, no one questioned how I was going to manage the household. I just did. Everyone moved on with their lives, and for a while, I was scared all of the time. How was I going to make it through the month financially, how was I going to go through all of this stuff, how was I going to make it? I did most all of this—on my own (with God). I came into a strength, which no one ever really acknowledged, even I was not aware of at the time. How interesting it is that now you question my strength and ability to manage a household.

I am not blind to my decision, in fact my eyes have been opened to a love which I can see, which is tangible, which will sustain Barton & I through the hardships and joys. When you asked me to define soul mate, I didn't know how to define it to you because it goes deeper than the romanticized "soul mate" in love poems. What are we, really, beyond bones, blood, thinking mind? What is the soul? Is the soul a part of God? So if you believe God is outside of our being, the definition would be different than if you see God in each of us. I could say, and do, that I have found my "Adam," my other half which completes my being, a piece of God, but that would make no sense to you if you see the body or the soul just as flesh or just as the psychology of the mind.

I was disappointed that you did not come to Purification and I hope you will consider coming to the one April 30-May 1 for several reasons. It will give you an understanding of the language and level of the spiritual foundation that will outlast the tangible fragility of our lives (Barton & I as well as all of us), and the support and network of this family. And you will see me in a role of a woman, healer, teacher, adult, and protector instead of as a girl, which is probably a bit scary for any parent but necessary if you are to see the strength, capability and ability to which you question both Barton and I. In fact, it would be great if Linda and Scott could all come to experience the weekend, it would be such a connecting experience.

I have not chosen an easy path, but my life has never been easy, from the day I was born, and even before that. I am now just beginning to understand why & the work, the soul work there is to do. I hope this gives some insight into our relationship & a few of the specifics of the logistics. I realize I cannot calm or relieve all of your fears. I am not fearful of the future nor of my life with Barton, we are ready to begin our lives together.

With Love,

Megan

In March, we traveled to Chicago for Barton's spring break so that I could meet his father and stepmother, Nancy for the first time as well. They met us in baggage claim, and since it was in the evening, we drove to a pizzeria.

I noticed how Barton's dad, Stan had the exact same facial expressions as Barton, especially when Barton is puzzled or frustrated. The running joke in the family is that Barton had his father's genes and would lose his hair by the time he was age 30. Barton's bushy eyebrows were an exact match to his father's, which furled to display what were clearly deep thoughts.

Nancy looked so similar to my own stepmother, classy and professional, right down to the business suit.

As we sat down at our table, I distinctly heard Nancy comment, "I think it's great that you two want to be together, but I think you should have a commitment ceremony, not a wedding."

I looked at Barton. My mouth wouldn't move. What could I say to that? How could I even respond? If I protested, it might cause further conflict, but if I didn't, I was being rude. I thought for a moment, but there wasn't anything I could do but listen.

She went on, "It's almost the same as a wedding, just without the legal aspects. That way, Barton could keep his benefits."

Barton chimed in, "We're getting married. Period. I understand and appreciate your concern, but we are fully aware of what this means and we will make it work."

Stan leaned back in his chair, "We're happy to support you however we can. We just want to make sure that you don't get penalized if you don't need to be."

In the same way that I heard Stan and Nancy worrying over the loss of Barton's benefits, I knew as well that my father had been concerned about our relationship and our marriage. I had heard these words before.

Barton kept ordering root beers, but I wasn't going to turn down Nancy's offer for a glass of wine. A feeling of awkwardness rose from the table, and I thought it best to smile and chew on pizza crust.

Barton couldn't stop smiling, and when I picked up a piece of pizza to put it into his mouth, I had to wait. Later, Barton noted how his dad didn't know what to do since he was the one who always helped Barton eat.

"I think he felt displaced," Barton said, "He was clearly excited to see me so happy and in love. At the same time, he wasn't sure how to express it."

The rest of the week, I was terrified and tried to avoid any further conversation of commitment ceremony verses marriage ceremony. I met several extended family members, but putting names to faces was just a blur for me then.

Over the next few months, I would begin putting the pieces together as to Barton's family dynamics and how I would fit within them.

Barton's family dynamics resembled my own, and yet we had different experiences growing up. While my parents were divorced when I was three, his were divorced when Barton was eleven. While I spent years switching back and forth between houses, Barton refused and his mom also recognized how hard it would be to go back and forth between parents, so he spent much of his teenage years with his father. Both our fathers were remarried, and we both spent many years pushing our stepmothers away.

At first, I wasn't sure how to step into Barton's family, so I tiptoed through family dinners, quietly showing only my gracious Southern charm, leaving my own colorful personality and mischievousness for when Barton and I were alone.

Between the first meeting and the wedding, I was trying to keep up with who was married to who. It wasn't until much later, after my first trip to the mountains in Randolph, New Hampshire after we were married, that I was able to meet many of Barton's family members on a more intimate level than just putting names and faces together.

That same spring, my cousin was getting married in Pensacola, Florida. At this point, I was still trying to take advantage of every opportunity for Barton to meet and spend time with my family. I was nervous since this was the first time many of my extended family members would meet Barton.

I didn't know how they would react to Barton being in a wheelchair, and I was an anxious mess making the seven-hour trip. Not only was I frantic about directions, constantly questioning whether we were headed in the right direction, but I sped most of the way. As we passed through one of the small towns in Southern Alabama, I was stopped by the local police for going 55 in a 35-mile per hour zone. Standing at my window, he was about to write a ticket when he glanced in the backseat at Barton's wheelchair, and let us off with a warning. This only escalated my tension.

Barton laughed, "See, there's no need to worry about the little stuff when you have me around."

When we arrived, my father met us in the lobby and helped us get settled in the hotel. At the church before the wedding, my father and uncle showed Barton the long line of Methodist ministers in my family history. We wove through small corridors to get a glimpse of my ancestry.

At the wedding reception, I decided no matter what, we were going to have a good time and celebrate. As the music played, Barton stood up from his wheelchair, and we enjoyed dancing through several slow songs. I closed my eyes, letting go of the anxiety of whether extended family members would accept us.

I didn't realize how our dancing was an opportunity for my family to see Barton and me in a relaxed setting, to see the connection between us. I wasn't sure anyone knew Barton could stand or that we could dance together. No, I wasn't his caretaker; Barton was clearly in love, holding and supporting me, as I was him.

Later, I was perched on Barton's lap, sipping a cocktail, at a table with my aunts and cousins.

"Barton just graduated from school in Tucson. In fact, we're going back this week to visit with friends and for a martial arts seminar. At the moment, we're planning to get married in November. And we're looking to move, maybe to Birmingham. We haven't decided yet."

Later, my aunt would comment how special it was to see Barton and me together.

I think on some level we scared our families by continually stepping out there, without fully knowing what the result will be. We have shown that we will live through whatever challenges we face; we will survive and we will thrive. So, our families have shifted and grown as we have.

We knew what we were going to do, and no one could change our plans. I stood my ground; after all, I did inherit those stubborn genes, as did Barton. The power of love was just too great to back down.

Moon Scenes

2.

Waltzing by Wave

*We stir to dance, our feet pliant, burrowing
warm into the softness of an evening sand.
The languishing waves murmur
a cadence like nimble fingers
subtle upon piano keys.
Your piña scent melts like honey on my tongue.
I move to you like a timid boatman,
his masts ravished by the winds.
Dusk is past and the sea clings to the shore,
taunting. Still, I sway to the linger of sun, ever fresh,
in the bright of your eye.*

~ S. Barton Cutter, November 2004

Chapter Six

Waltzing at the Edge of Creation

Together, we waltz at the cusp
of creation.
With all my love, B.

~ S. Barton Cutter, May 2003

When I introduced Megan to my dad and stepmother, the first words from my stepmother's mouth were, "I think you should have a commitment ceremony rather than getting married."

For many, a commitment ceremony is used to ensure the comfort and security of people with disabilities maintaining their individual government benefits. For me, however, agreeing to a commitment ceremony instead of a full marriage would have been an easy out.

While my stepmother meant well, a simple commitment ceremony represented to me an unwillingness to accept and engage in the responsibilities of marriage, both spiritually and secularly.

As a person with a disability, it has been ingrained in me from a young age that retaining government benefits, such as Social Security Income and Social Security Disability Income, were the be all and end all. Because of the variety of challenges associated with forging a life that would provide me with the greatest independence possible, including a way for me to live on my own, acquire the necessary support and transportation, and find sustainable work, it was always assumed federal benefits were the only realistic option.

For my parents, the idea I could earn a living greater than what Social Security could offer me was, in many ways, beyond comprehension. I didn't discover until many years later how profoundly this impacted my father. As, for him, not only was it a concern over how much income I could generate for my family, but it was also the extreme transformation that I had undergone during my years away at college.

To him, there was little I was willing to take on, especially in high school when, despite my capabilities, I would often refuse to do something as simple as drive my own wheelchair. He was not there for the beginnings of my metamorphosis that began moments after he left me in my college dorm when, after a brief moment of mourning, I had a neighbor pack several books in my bag and I took off to the middle of the quad, identified the cutest co-ed in sight and proceeded to ask if she would assist me in turning the pages as I studied. Nor was he present as simple choices like this gradually taught me my own capacity for self-reliance.

As I grew into adulthood, I found that the attempt at mitigating risk through Social Security Disability Income served as an unnecessary crutch; one that stifled the opportunities for growth which lay before me.

Marriage was the biggest of these, and, while there may have been other ways to honor our commitment of love to one another, legal marriage alone clarified to the world the responsibilities that we were accepting for one another. Not only as a newly wedded husband and wife, but also for me, as a whole man dedicated to taking care of his wife at every level.

I found it necessary to clarify my willingness to take a stand physically and spiritually to serve, protect and provide for our family.

Since I stood and walked for the first time publically in completion of my apprenticeship as healer, it only seemed natural, that I would also stand and walk in service to and in honor of my new wife and family.

In the year between completing my apprenticeship and preparing for our marriage, training in budo taijutsu took on a new meaning for me.

During that year, I focused heavily on physical exercise and building core muscle so that my body could stand straighter and more aligned with my spirit.

I also found a walker that enabled me to work on standing and walking without the immediate support of another person. This combination of increased physical alignment and an ever-growing sense of independence served as a way for me to hold an open connection throughout the course of our wedding ceremony and later, our lives together.

As I was working to develop my capacity to stand, I found myself making a conscious decision not to speak of this work with anyone beyond Megan and those who were directly involved in helping me accomplish this goal.

Part of this decision stemmed from an understanding that in order to succeed, it was imperative that I minimize the voices and opinions of those around me. On many levels, the physical act of standing and walking flew in the face of the accepted definition of disability. In particular, it defied the accepted definition of what was possible for someone with my particular degree of Cerebral Palsy.

Megan

I had seen brides carry an organizational bridal book in their hands, and now I was one of them. In my white three-ring binder bursting at the seams, I gathered swatches of fabric, reception menus, names for the guest list, an outline of the wedding week's to-do list, and more.

Yes, my father gifted us a beautiful wedding. I knew early on that budgeting would be part of the planning, and when I went to him with two or three estimates for each wedding service venue, he graciously agreed, "You're doing your own research. I trust you."

Within reason, we had the freedom to create the ceremony we had dreamed of, and for the most part, Barton and I agreed on what we wanted to do.

However, the day I sat down with a calendar to talk about dates with several schedules in my hands, including the University of Alabama football calendar, Barton balked, "You've got to be kidding! Why do we need the football schedule?"

(handwritten: Indeed!)

It was a challenge to convey how prominent football culture was in a small southern town. On home game weekends, the town was overrun by RV's, tailgate parties and hours of standstill traffic. If we even considered having the wedding on a game day, no one would come, traffic and parking would be a nightmare, and we would have to have a TV in the backroom, as my father and stepmother did during their wedding—scheduled for the exact time of the Auburn-Alabama rivalry football game.

No matter how hard I tried to explain that those die-hard football fans would choose a game over a wedding, my words were met with Barton's laugh and rolling eyes.

To avoid any conflict, however, Barton and I settled on what promised to be a perfect fall day where there were no martial arts training seminars or football games.

Our guest list became longer and longer as we combined our family and community circles. Both of our fathers' sides of the family were overflowing with more than 50 people each, a smaller contingent from our mothers' sides, family that came from abroad, our training family, my work friends, creative writing group, and our personal friends. We knew that it was important to invite those who had supported us individually and as a couple.

Once a date had been set, I felt the joy of opening the sealed box with the wedding dress folded inside. Alone in my bedroom, I slipped it on, and was delighted that it still fit. Feeling the lace touch my skin and gathering the long train around my feet made me glow from within.

However, I did go shopping with Linda and Nancy for the rehearsal dinner dress. Our families met in Birmingham to discuss wedding details, and the second dress I tried was a perfect sky blue gown with sequin top, which wrapped around my neck. I didn't want to take it off.

Outside the dressing room, though, I could hear the excitement from both stepmothers as they searched for different styles and shades of fabric. I realized how similar both Linda and Nancy were, and they made a great pair together. This was the perfect opportunity for our families to connect, and I wasn't about to disrupt the energy of the moment.

I tried on many more dresses before picking out the blue gown from underneath the pile and coming out of the dressing room with a smile across my face, "It's this one."

While we had been shopping for dresses, Barton, his father and my father went to see the Civil Rights Museum in Birmingham, and later we all met back up to enjoy a lovely engagement dinner at a seafood restaurant.

With most important decisions out of the way, we could now focus on other details. We were privileged in that we designed our own wedding rings.

I knew a local jeweler who designed rings, and we both had something specific in mind for our wedding bands. We sat at table in the middle of the shop and began to describe what each of us had envisioned. Jacob, the owner, took notes and made suggestions.

Both bands would be made of white gold with four crosses on the cardinal directions. My ring would be small and smooth, while Barton's ring would be thicker and more masculine.

We returned several times to watch as the pieces of our rings were melded together, before the polishing stages. We watched as tiny fragments of a cross were shown to us.

Jacob mentioned, "I rarely allow people to see the unfinished pieces. Many people can't seem to appreciate the unfinished product, and the transformation that these metals go through to become the beautiful piece of jewelry that you receive."

On our final visit, we beamed over the two bands, which were polished and complete. We tried them on, and Jacob even took pictures of our hands interweaving with bands sparkling side by side.

Other friends would come together in helping me organize our wedding such as Cindy, who would do the calligraphy on the envelopes for our wedding invitations, Ron, a co-worker, who did our photography and a local florist who would make the bouquet exactly how I envisioned it.

Truly, we were able to make our marriage ceremony our own; it made all the difference being able to celebrate our personal style.

The week before the wedding I was in the midst of a flurry of details making packages for family coming in, gathering travel plans, and last minute errands.

Betsy, my matron of honor and Catherine came two days before the ceremony, and accompanied me to have our nails done, visit the church, and copy programs the day before the wedding. Virginia came as well, and I was humbled when she took up a broom to clean the student center, which would be transformed into the reception hall. Several members of my family had decorated the reception tables with decorations I had gathered, blue candles, bowls with white and blue pebbles, and poems that Barton and I had composed for each other.

Our families came together and did all they could to make the day exceptional.

While my excitement was on overdrive for most of our engagement, I noticed that a week or two prior to the ceremony, as plans became finalized and the organizational aspects of the ceremony took shape, my anticipation became even more palpable. Larry, Fred and Al, students in budo taijutsu, had agreed to build a ramp to provide me access to the church altar. As this neared completion, I began to notice new ways in which our community supported us.

Larry had taken it upon himself not only to help build the ramp for me—a vital part of ensuring that Megan and I could have the physical logistics function as we had hoped, but he also spent long hours exercising with me and helping me discover the balance I needed to stand.

At the same time, I witnessed a coming together of our family and friends to support and share with us in our union. Some of my closest men friends, Neal, Dean, and Alan gathered with me in our living room and laughed at how my connection with Megan had grown over the last two years to envelop everyone we talked to.

I came to see who, within our various circles, valued the growth of both Megan and me, and who did not. In particular, a close childhood friend who I had invited to be one of my groomsmen phoned the day before the rehearsal to inform me that he would be unable to attend.

"Barton, I was on the way to the airport, and I got called into work. I won't be able to come tomorrow either. They don't have anyone to cover for me."

This would have seemed like a perfectly reasonable issue, but Tom was the type of person who, for as long as I could remember, bailed at the last minute, particularly when the spotlight was to be on someone other than him.

The phone call replayed in my head like an all too familiar melody. I was disappointed that he couldn't be there and even more disappointed to see that he had not changed after many years. At the same time, it helped me differentiate the numerous transformations I had undergone. I asked Bill, who knew us well from training and understood the depth of connection I had developed with Megan.

After the rehearsal, we gathered wedding party and guests alike at one of Tuscaloosa's finest banquet halls sharing drink and feast. This was, I believe, the only moment throughout the weekend where both Megan and I were able to fully enjoy the company of others without being enraptured with one another to the exclusion of others.

Before Megan arrived, I gathered with three of my favorite cousins, Simone, Jill and Justin, who was my groomsman who traveled from England to stand by my side. We chuckled over how I, the youngest of our generation, had somehow beaten the three of them to marriage, in a healthy dose of cousinly jest. We also loved Simone's attempt to disguise her broken ankle with an elegant evening gown and makeshift accessories.

Over cocktails, we spent time side by side in a combination of chatting with cousins and family, and meeting additional members of one another's families.

For me, the most profound moment of the evening was the video that Megan's father made with a montage of photos of both Megan and me growing up and finding one another. While the video was exquisite, what brought me to tears were the words of Louis in his introductory toast.

> Megan and Barton, Your two families and friends who love you are here to celebrate your marriage. You have done the easy part. You have found each other, fallen in love and are committing to the journey together through life in this marriage. While God accepts you as you are, God is not finished with you yet! Marriage takes ongoing hard work and you have to commit to work on your relationship. Remember that when your partner is having a hard time you may have something to do with it even though you may not be responsible for it. Marriage is that experience of caring, sharing and loving in which you grow to become more of the person you are meant to be in this life.

Having been uncertain if I was the best match for his daughter only months before, I was amazed at his recognition and validation of how happy we made one another. Moreover, I was humbled by his loving invitation into the Clan McLeod and his willingness to learn from our love for each other and let go of his own fear through the acknowledgement of our connection.

We had both left the rehearsal dinner separately for a night on the town with our bridesmaids and groomsmen, many from out of town. I hadn't really thought about where I would sleep that night, and I ended up sharing a hotel room with one of my bridesmaids. I was so elated and wound up that at 2:30 am, I was still wide-awake. I wasn't nervous, just purely excited, as this was my wedding day.

On our honeymoon, Barton would share how his evening out with the guys prompted him to call his mother first thing and request an extra large cup of coffee and a healthy dose of aspirin.

The morning of the wedding, Linda and her sister Bryna, hosted a breakfast for all of the bridesmaids. All seven bridesmaids and my immediate family gathered in Linda's hotel room. I opened a few gifts—one was a stuffed doll that sang, *"We're going to the chapel, and we're gonna get married."*

There were boxes of luxurious lingerie, and we all giggled about the fun on my wedding night.

Though, I did get a bit carried away. When Judy made a comment, I snapped back, "Well, why are we talking about you? This is my wedding day."

As soon as the words came out of my mouth, I felt guilty, but I was so wrapped up in the moment about my day, my time. The awkwardness passed, and after the wedding, I would apologize for letting my ego get the best of me.

Then we were all off in a hurry to get our hair and make-up done at a local hairdresser. We all took turns having our hair done, and before I knew it, I found myself wearing way more make-up than I had ever put on my face in my life. I would have chosen something subtler, but again, I was caught up in the moment of glitz and glamour.

We all hurried back to the church to change into our wedding attire. I had so many bridesmaids, seven in all; the chatter of getting ready was a hum of excitement that charged the air. We were pulling and tugging dresses on, fixing hair, and the buzz of all of us drifted through the church halls.

When all of the bridesmaids had left to take pictures in the sanctuary of the church, I found myself alone in the dressing room. I looked at myself in the mirror, a bride on her wedding day, and I could feel my mother around me, blessing me. It was an extraordinary moment. Having such an intimate moment with my mother was unfamiliar, and I felt myself needing to have another physical presence in the room.

"Do you know where Linda is?" I asked someone in the hallway. While they went to find her, I waited outside the dressing room.

Eventually, Linda came to greet me, but soon after, I was whisked away for pictures in the sanctuary.

After preliminary photographs were taken, we congregated back in the dressing room, a circle of women. I sat down for a few minutes, the puff of white lace and fabric encircling me. We waited for the priest to get us when the time arrived, and he came in with a pre-wedding blessing and prayer.

While my bridesmaids made their way down the church aisle, I was standing in the hallway with my father.

"Megan, this goes so fast. I am so proud of you, and I want you to remember every part of it. When you are walking down the aisle, I hope you will look at each person who has supported you."

I am so appreciative of his words because I do remember every aspect of our wedding, and those who support us as a couple together. As I walked down the aisle holding onto my father's arm, I made eye contact with our many friends and family who had gathered.

I looked ahead of me, Barton standing in his walker on the aisle, dazzling in a white tuxedo and sky-blue vest and bow tie. My father gave his official blessing. I walked up the ramp to the altar and stood beside Barton.

Perhaps the most profound aspect of our marriage ceremony was our decision to write our own vows. Prior to the ceremony, I spent a lot of time in silence identifying exactly what it was that I wanted to vow. I felt there were specific pieces about how I saw my role as a husband that needed to be formalized and that were not covered to the same depth in the traditional vows of the church. I wrote them, little by little, perhaps one vow every day or every other day over the period of a week or so. I was deliberate not to force them but rather hold a concept and sit with it until the appropriate words came. I stopped several times because I wanted to get it out, but it wasn't ready.

In this way, my vows became a statement that encapsulated both personal values for my role in our relationship and an expression of how I understood love to flow between and from ourselves.

As such, I was determined to speak all of these vows I had prepared. During the ceremony, however, when the time came, I had already been on my feet for a good 30 minutes, and the priest recognized it was unlikely I would make it through all of them. He selected the first three and then the last one for me to recite. While I knew how out of breath I was, I was caught off guard by the abbreviation and made a point, after the ceremony, to ensure that Megan understood all of them in their entirety.

Standing face to face with my love and mustering every ounce of energy to speak the words clearly, I felt my entire being tremble with the resonance of these words as they came forth.

As Megan turned to share her vows, all I can recall is gazing into the rich chocolate of her deep and loving eyes, and the sound of her voice, soft against my baritone pulse. Ironically, grasping the actual words she spoke eluded me, for all I felt was the emanation of her love.

> Megan My love, I take thee to be my wife.
>
> Like a pillar, I will stand solid as Marble carved by divine implement. Because of love, we shall not fall.
>
> Our foundation is above and, from this, we may build.
>
> Forever I shall serve you
>
> as I serve God: with all my soul for it is His grace which brought us together like two galaxies spinning into one.
>
> Forever shall I love you
>
> for you are the one whom my soul remembers and together we are made whole.
>
> Forever shall I strive
>
> to be a clearer instrument for God that this clarity be

reflected in our family like the sun radiant on water at dawn.

Forever shall I be with you

for all that I am is now yours and you shall never be alone.

Forever shall I be humbled by you

for out of you will grow our family like pines springing forth from warm clay.

Forever shall I protect you

for without you there is no purpose in manhood, like a body, cold, without breath.

Forever shall I provide for you

for with sustenance comes life, like the sun melting the frozen sea.

Our abodes which were separate are now one and one shall not be divided. As drops of rain are one in the stream, so are we one in service and love.

Megan

Barton,

You stand before me as a man,

and I take you as my husband.

God has brought us together,

Love has connected us,

together, we are one.

In laughter and in tears,

as the morning breaks to

the setting of the sun,

We are one.

As you stand here before me,

I stand before you-

grounding and strong, as the roots of a tree.

I am humbled before you,

I will persevere through hardships,

bending and flexing like a reed in a storm.

I will nurture our children, raise them well,

as they are the future.

As rays of sun sparkle

with drops of rain, making rainbows.

I trust you, and I love you.

This is my solemn vow.

My grandfather, a Methodist Minister gave the sermon, and my aunt's brother-in-law, who was an Episcopal Priest, stood on the altar as well. Judy made bread and wine for communion, a true gift of love used for the ceremony.

Barton used a stick wrapped with ribbon to slide the ring onto my finger, and he stood at the altar for most of the ceremony, with the exception of taking communion. But, to me the most adventuresome and holy of events was walking out of the church, with my husband.

None of Barton's family knew that he was planning to walk me out until the rehearsal. During the rehearsal, we were both getting used to the slope of the ramp and Barton's walker. At first, his feet slipped under, not able to keep balance.

By the time the actual wedding ceremony was over, Barton had been standing for about 45 minutes straight; he was already exhausted.

But when the recessional music began, the energy of the moment and our newly formed connection as husband and wife carried our bodies down the aisle as divine energy flowed through us.

The walk out of the church with my husband was electrifying. Barton used his walker down the ramp, and there was not one misstep down the ramp and past our families and friends who watched in amazement.

As we walked out of the doors, we all let out a huge scream of excitement, as we heard clapping from family and friends inside the church.

Taking my first steps from the altar, I felt the muscles in my legs quivering with exhaustion. The perfect placement of each step was made only by the flow of love coursing between Megan and me. Making our way down the central aisle, the physical sensation left my awareness and I found myself in a focused state led only by the rhythmic pulse of my heart and the sound of my feet touching the floor.

When we reached the entrance to the church, our recession came to a close. Megan, Betsy and the rest of her bridesmaids screamed with delight. Despite my internal elation, my intense concentration and exhaustion left little room for external expression. In fact, when Megan later mentioned to me the uproar of applause that followed our exit, I had no recollection.

In retrospect, I realized that I was so focused on Megan during and after our wedding ceremony that I was only vaguely aware of all of those who were cheering for us inside the church.

Though, over the course of the weekend, my focus shifted and the profundity of those who gathered around us in love overwhelmed me.

When we arrived at the reception and it came time for Megan and me to have our first dance as a married couple, I was once again on my feet and ready to swing my beautiful bride about the dance floor. Okay, perhaps not, but there was no hesitation when I stood to embrace Megan, swaying back and forth with the melody of *Fields of*

Gold in the background.

I recall a lightness in the soles of my feet holding Megan in my arms. Weight shifting from one foot to the other, my arms found the golden softness of Megan's neck. It took all of my might not to lose myself in the sweet nectar of her perfumed skin, and I alternated stealing pecks on her lips and reflecting back the admiration of those who stood watching us.

Later I would ask Megan about who had taken the lead during the dance. She paused and a smile grew across her quasi-innocent face, "You did; I felt you. There's no doubt in my mind that you led."

During our dance, I caught a glimpse of the others encircling the dance floor. I also noticed my Aunt Jackie reading a poem that Megan and I had written together and set out on the tables. Jackie was crying.

After the first set of dances, we all gathered for a round of toasts. When immediate family and friends were done, Barton began his toast by thanking those who came. April was standing right beside him, and he thanked her for working with him on standing and walking.

I held it together until this moment, when tears broke free. Someone handed me a tissue, and I wiped my eyes.

Like all weddings, the reception was full of fun, pictures, and conversations, and we delighted at bringing different communities together that would have never normally met or mingled.

Later, when we were ushered to cut the cake, Barton and I held the knife together, cutting into the cake. I put a piece in my mouth; my matron of honor whispered, "You are supposed to give it to him."

"I am," was my response as I gave him a huge kiss and exchanged the sweetness of the cake. Then he did the same.

No, Barton can't lift a spoon to give me a bite of some delicious dessert, but from the first weekend we were together, we would exchange bites of chocolate through a kiss. Sensual and intimate, we normally kept these moments private. It just seemed right that we should do the same here, taking care to feed each other wedding cake in a way that was natural to us.

After I had thrown the bouquet of flowers, it was now time for Barton to remove my garter.

Judy had always joked about making a garter for me that Barton could remove easily, and I was giddy when I discovered she had altered the garter. She had added velcro with a string that Barton could gently pull with his teeth, and take the garter off. He then flung it to the awaiting bachelors.

After the official ceremonies of the wedding reception were complete, we danced the night away with friends and family.

Leaving the church, those in the wedding and some friends from out of town headed to a local pizza restaurant for another round of conversation, laughter and celebration. Having not eaten much at the reception, pizza smelled delightful.

We celebrated with friends until late in the evening. While the ceremony was over, it was just the beginning of our journey.

On our honeymoon, we divided our week in half. The first half of the week, I gifted Megan with the deep blue of the Gulf of Mexico and the soft white sands of the Florida beaches where we spent from dawn until dusk burying our feet and wheels in the sands of the shore's edge. Megan's gentle spirit and understated strength were reflected to me in the clear shimmering waters of the Gulf at sunset.

I knew this place well as it was a regular vacation spot during my youth, and thought it the ideal honeymoon locale to begin our lives together. I trusted the staff at one particular resort. Not only would there be the ambiance of unending elegance that is befitting of any honeymoon, but the hotel staff would help me get from place to place giving Megan the chance to relax in a way that was not a typical occurrence.

We sat on those beaches, mingling toes and sand with the salt of an unending ocean, there was a taste of a poignant potentiality. The ceaseless ebb and flow of the ocean gives rise to the sacred flow of energies, the female form emerging formless from the primordial undercurrents into the crests of each wave. At the time, we were unaware of what was being revealed over that brief trip to the beach. Watching the quiet and seamless molding of waves from the ocean's unknowable depths became an iconic image for Megan's vast strength over the years to come.

While I knew Barton was planning our honeymoon according to the days I had off work, one of my co-workers suggested that I should take the whole week off. Doing everything I could to get the extra days, we began thinking about what we would like to do after our trip to Florida.

In a streak of good luck, our flight went through Atlanta. Instead of returning to Alabama, we stepped off the plane in Atlanta and drove into the north Georgia mountains to a cabin sitting over a stream. When I was a child, my dad, stepmother and I slept on the floor listening to the rain on the tin roof above. The three of us would make ice cream, sit and read on the back porch, and walk through the overgrown trails behind the cabin. When I brought my friends, we stayed in the loft and snickered up all night telling secrets and girl talk.

This kind of peacefulness and fun I wanted to share with Barton as we began our marriage. When we arrived at the cabin just before sunset, the ground was wet from an afternoon storm, and the stairs leading up to the porch were slick. Carefully, I turned Barton's wheel-chair around, and carefully rolled his wheelchair each step, gaining footing before moving to the next one.

It was nearly impossible to get into any of the bedrooms because the hallway was so tiny, and I didn't feel like dragging Barton around. Instead, we built a fire in the woodstove burner in the main room and cuddled on the couch.

I did end up sliding down the slippery porch stairs once, with Barton in tow. Barton's wheelchair handlebar caught me right in the groin, and Barton also pulled a muscle. For the day, we nursed our wounds as we snuggled up on the sofa, reading poetry to each other.

One afternoon, we were adventurous and took a walk as far as the trail would take us, along a stream into the woods. Barton laughed while I shook off the spider webs I kept walking into. We made our way back, delighting in the sanctuary of the woods, listening to the brook, and eventually finding stillness as we sat together on the porch staring into the forest.

My father and stepmother had stayed at the cabin the weekend before we arrive, and left a bottle of champagne and a gift card so that we could have dinner at a retreat center nestled in the north Georgia pines.

We drove through tight and winding mountain roads that led to this spectacular resort tucked away from view. Once we arrived at the retreat center, we wandered around wooden pathways while we waited for our reservation. Chilly from the cold mountain air, we warmed ourselves in front of a stone fireplace before sitting down in the rustic dining room, tasting fresh steak and salmon with our bottle of champagne.

Later, I would discover Barton's connection to the mountains, spending summers on the porch watching storms drift over the mountain ridge. I had always felt the solidity of Barton's spirit underneath the uncertainty of our lives.

From the vantage of a mountain peak, Barton sees everything that lies above and below. From lightening storms, clear skies with dancing stars, boulders rolling down to valleys below, and the land spreading to the horizon, Barton's strength has been to see where we need to go in order to sustain our family, what roadblocks may be ahead, and to identify clear paths around them.

Barton has this quality of being able to jump into the unknown, with a grounded sense that no matter what happens, we would land on solid ground. The mountain bedrock remains and yet the landscape is slowly etched over time, and I have felt Barton's fundamental fortitude endure.

Morning Stroll

The chilled air greets my breath,
clouds shown pristine in sun fade
like a tapped-out mine of images;
cherished nugget carried away by thirsting of gain
or gusting winds.

Dogs, scrambling for a robin
stumble dumbfounded to a resigned halt
gaping at her escape-
a string of dawn warms our backs.

~ S. Barton Cutter

I feel you behind me,
the warmth of your hand
soaking through my skin
like a lavender bath.

We have known each other
for a long time, you and I.

Golden petals
fall around us
as we dance in the twilight.
Fingers slip through
each other and around.

We look into each other's souls
and melt the darkness of the night
into the dawn of a new day.

~Megan M. Cutter, 2003

Chapter Seven

Moving in the Midst of a Hurricane

Six months before the wedding, Barton wasted no time making the three-day trip to Tuscaloosa, Alabama with his father, not even waiting for graduation day from the University of Arizona in Tucson. We were lucky that I was living in my mother's house, which was a one-level ranch style house, and, while I had an entire house of my mother's furnishings, everything that Barton owned fit into a white van. When Barton moved in, we went through the process of creating our home together by merging our two lives.

As the summer went on, I saw Barton go through a difficult transition because Tuscaloosa was not the most accessible place in the country. In fact, Barton could hardly get out of the front door. There were no sidewalks, even on some of the major roads around our house. The bus system was not accessible either; Barton could have only received accessible bus service for a few hours each day, and the bus stop was several miles away in a rough part of town.

He was becoming more agitated. This was not Barton's style, to rely on others so much in order to get around. It was clear we needed to move. But where?

We considered Birmingham, which also had accessibility issues, so we began to look out of state. When we talked about moving, we took into consideration housing, transportation, community support and job opportunities, all a tall order. We didn't want to live in a big city like Atlanta or Washington DC, but we also needed a town big enough with public transportation and other support services.

Another factor we considered was my work schedule and the inflexibilities that came with the position.

In fact, my workload had tripled because of additional responsibilities, which raised my stress-level to almost unbearable heights. We both knew it was time to move on, so while I was at work, Barton began to research and consider our options. Thus began a complex issue of underground research.

Tuscaloosa was, after all, a small town where people talk. So when I found out that four or five members of a local service organization associated with my work lived in our neighborhood, I was cautious. My neighbors were intrigued by the fact that I would marry someone with a disability, and the line between my work and personal life quickly began to blend.

At the time, Barton would walk our new puppy Bear around the block. This not only gave him an opportunity to get out of the house, he would also talk with neighbors to find out what was going on.

At a business luncheon in May, I was sitting with several colleagues from the office. I was already upset because of a shipping crisis that morning. One of my neighbors sitting at the other end of the table burst out, "Megan, you and Barton aren't moving in September are you?"

Everyone looked directly at me. The cat was out of the bag. I could feel my face getting flushed and the tears brimming.

Shaking, I nearly crawled under the table.

"No, not yet," was all I could say. In tears, I tore out of the luncheon.

How horrible it was to go to each of those co-workers and backtrack my way out of things. Walking into a colleague's office, my hands were shaking as I shut the door.

"We don't really know what our plans are. Barton's trying to find work here, and we're just keeping all of our options open."

Breathlessly, I left; my stomach in a tight ball. I felt ill the rest of the day.

Since my neighbors knew information about our move to North Carolina that I could not share with my company, this provided a great deal of internal conflict and external drama.

After traveling to Durham in the spring of 2004, Barton and I thought of Raleigh as having great potential for our move. There was an arts community, job opportunities, and a well-connected disability community. There were still missing pieces—health insurance, a place to live, and a secure position.

We would have temporary insurance for a limited amount of time when I left my corporate job. I was afraid that if they knew that I was leaving before handing in a formal resignation, there would be consequences leaving us without options for health insurance.

In fact, the fear of anyone finding out I would leave caused much anxiety for the last six months I worked there and was only magnified with the neighborly connections. I was so vigilant, that to many of our friends, it seemed like we just picked up and left.

Barton and I would both need to find work, which was difficult being out of state. Barton started working on a writing contract in North Carolina, and shortly after that, he was toying with how we could create our own writing business. We were always doing small contract writing jobs on the side, and it made sense to formalize this work.

In early August, Barton was attending a conference in Raleigh, and we found an apartment complex that had a space available in October. We made a plan to move by the fall. This would give me time to prepare my work, fix my mother's house to put it up for sale, and establish the connections for the move.

I will never forget picking up the phone at work. Barton was on the other line, "We're moving," he said.

"Yes, and," my voice tapered off, distracted by the piles of paperwork in front of me.

"September 1, we're moving," he breathed into the phone. Time slowed. People walking in front of the window in my office blurred together. What? I looked at the calendar and calculated. September first was less than three weeks away.

"Okay," I said is a calm voice.

Barton explained the apartment complex had an accessible apartment with larger doorways and a larger bathroom. He couldn't say no. I couldn't either, following with another, "Okay."

I hung up the phone. We were moving, across state lines, in less than one month.

Overnight, my to-do list ran off the page in preparation for our move. I chose not to tell anyone at work about the move until September 1st because our health insurance would cover us through the end of the month.

We needed to get Barton moved to North Carolina on September 1st, the house packed and ready to sell, and I needed to prepare my resignation.

We did tell our close family and friends we were moving. Some of them were concerned since neither one of us had a permanent position waiting for us in North Carolina. How would we manage? All we knew is that Tuscaloosa wasn't working for us, and in order to sustain our family, we had to leave.

On my birthday, we had heard that Hurricane Katrina was headed for New Orleans. Barton had a doctor's appointment in Birmingham that morning, and our plans were to take off the rest of the afternoon to play in the city for my birthday. Driving to Birmingham, I remember looking outside at this greenish tint to the sky and shaking my head, "This is not good."

At the doctor's office, we listened to the news reports about Katrina hitting New Orleans. We decided to drive straight home, as Alabama was in the center of Katrina's path. I drove as fast as I could so we could prepare ourselves. The wind whipped the car across the road, and I gripped the steering wheel to keep control.

Early that night, I gasped when the tornado sirens went off. The interior bathroom was so small, we couldn't fit Barton inside.

We had been through these conversations before because emergency preparedness brings on a whole new meaning when you consider the needs of people with disabilities. If we had to evacuate, what would we need? How much backup medicine do we have? How do we move without the wheelchair? What do you need in an emergency grab bag besides medical information? What about flooding, accessibility for evacuation routes or emergency shelter? What is necessary and what can be left behind? The list of questions to answer and logistics to think about were endless.

As the tornado sirens went off that night, the best we could do is put Barton in his wheelchair blocking the doorway to the bathroom. The radio was blasting how the emergency station lost power. No one knew why the tornado sirens were going off, nor how long we should stay in our safe places. Later, we were told that the wind had hit over 70 miles per hour.

While the sirens were going off, the phone rang. I panicked. I practically climbed over Barton to get out of the bathroom. Thinking it might be my grandfather who lived only a mile away and was known to ignore the turbulent weather in Tuscaloosa, I raced into the bedroom to answer the phone.

Happy Birthday to you. Happy birthday to you. Happy birthday dear Megan, happy birthday to you. On the other end, my father, Linda and Scott had burst into full song.

Should I interrupt them? Should I hang up? It was a moment of pure irony. Finally, I broke in, "Gotta go, the tornado sirens are going off and we don't know why, and I'm in the bedroom."

That night, we slept in our clothes and boots just in case we needed to be on the move. While Tuscaloosa did not have any flooding, there were trees that fell on houses in our neighborhood. We spent the weekend cleaning up the neighborhood from the wind-blown trees and fallen brush.

Even though my grandfather was safe, he was without power for a week, while we had gotten power back the next day. Since he was such a stubborn man, I would bring a cooler with milk and orange juice to his house, sliding it into the doorway before he would get up in the mornings.

That Monday, there was an emergency meeting at work with local service organizations. I was asked to head up the publicity committee. My heart raced.

I fumbled, "I'd love to, but I think someone else would be better able to work with the media."

How could I say yes, when I knew that the next day, I would be walking in with my resignation letter? When I thought about it, I could hardly breathe. The rest of the day, I was so distracted, all I could do was shuffle paper from one pile to another, look over my task list, effectively accomplishing nothing at all.

The following morning, my heart pounded and my hands were shaking as I walked into my manager's office to break the news. It was thrilling and nerve-wracking at the same time.

There was no turning back now. I was leaving.

Since Barton had already left for Raleigh, I stayed behind to pack up the rest of the house, repair as much as I could and prepare my office for my departure. My manager worked out an arrangement for me to stay one week instead of the full two I had anticipated.

Katrina not only affected the coastline from Mississippi to Georgia, it had also knocked the oil pipelines out of service. After Barton left, there was much concern about how this might affect my getting up to Raleigh.

As I drove from home to work and back, the streets were empty. I was told not to waste gas by neighbors, and I would fill up after using just a gallon or two. Gas prices had risen to four and five dollars a gallon, and there was rationing at the gas stations. On the highway, if there was a gas truck, there was a whole line of cars trailing behind following it to its destination.

Everyone stayed at preparing for the worst. What if the pipelines didn't come back on? How would a town function? Gas was being siphoned out of cars, so I bought a gas-lock cap, made several home emergency boxes, and did not drive on the streets except to and from work. Since Barton had taken the television, I had no way of seeing the horrific pictures of the aftermath of Katrina.

Instead, I would stay up until one or two in the morning to paint the back steps, paint the front door, pack boxes, clean the house, and prepare for the move room by room. Exhausted by the full workload, my stress level rose as well. Were we making the right decision?

Many of our friends had loved ones who were affected by the hurricane, while others assisted in the recovery efforts. We left without saying goodbye to anyone. One day we were in Alabama. The next we were in North Carolina.

When I close my eyes,
I feel you caressing my skin,
a light touch on my cheek.
We move lightly at first,
barely touching the water with the tips
of our wings.
I melt into the sea as you lift
me out of my body.
We follow lightning into the skies
and gently fall as storm passes.
We glow like rainbows
streaking across dusk.
You let go gently,
and envelope me like the night.
For a long time
we do not move, you and I,
falling into each other's breath,
soaring over the moon-lit night.

~ Megan M. Cutter, 2004

Chapter Eight

This Ring I Carry Around My Neck

The ring I carried around my neck was too heavy for the tiny silver chain, making a sharp V at the base of my neck. The ring is a thick band of silver with four crosses on each cardinal point.

In the waiting room, Barton asked me to take his ring off and to keep it during his surgery. He gave a hug to his father and Nancy, who had flown in the night before.

When the nurses called his name, Barton asked me to take his ring off, and I slid it through the chain, attaching the clasp around my neck.

I knew that Barton had a Baclofen pump, a medical device that pumps medicine directly into his spinal cord to reduce his spasticity, and I knew that over the course of our marriage, he would have surgery to replace it every five to ten years. I had heard stories about Barton's muscles constricting to the point of shortening when he was a child, but he always talked about how training in martial arts combined with the pump changed all of this.

I found myself unprepared for this surgery, the first one since I had known Barton. I was unprepared for Barton's anxiety in the weeks prior, my list of what-if questions, and the help we would need after the surgery.

When we found out that Barton needed to have his pump replaced, he had just started a new job. To minimize the time he needed to recover at home, he planned to have surgery just before Christmas. Stan and Nancy flew in the evening before, and Barton's mother would wait until after Christmas. We thought we had everything planned, but I had no idea what to expect.

In the pre-op room, I wrangled Barton into a comfortable position on the gurney. This was a difficult feat since his legs wouldn't stay still, swaying from side to side from his spasms. Two nurses came and asked all of the standard questions before pulling out the needle to start an IV line. The first question Barton asked them is, "How is your aim?"

I held Barton's legs down while the nurses searched his arms for a good vein, poking him five times before finally hitting the vein. They wrapped tape over the line of fluid so it wouldn't come out before or during surgery, since Barton's arms increased their movement from his nervousness about the surgery.

Once the IV line had started dripping medication, Barton's muscles relaxed and he began to drift in and out of sleep. Stan would check in on us every once in a while, until Barton was feeling the full effects of the initial anesthetic.

After a few more kisses and taking turns saying "I love you" to each other, I left the pre-op room.

When I walked out, the nurse handed me a buzzer, the kind you receive when you are waiting at a restaurant. She told me, "You can go anywhere in the hospital, just don't leave the building. When this buzzer lights up or vibrates, come back to this desk, and the doctor will be ready to meet with you."

I made my way down to the cafeteria with Stan and Nancy. The three of us found a place to sit in the back of the cafeteria and pulled out our computers, making small talk. I slid the buzzer to the middle of the table. Still, I watched the clock on the bottom of my computer screen. The minutes ticked by. I was exhausted from finishing a project at 2:00 am the night before, and we made small talk while we were waiting.

As long and hard as I would stare at the buzzer, it still did not go off. How long was this going to take? I was an exhausted wreck.

Finally. Red flashing lights and pulsing vibrations rattled the table.

I leapt up. "I'll go."

I flew up the escalator, skipping every other step and was surprised to run face to face into Barton's doctor. "Barton is doing just fine. The surgery went well. During the surgery, we found the pump and the tubing were completely disconnected. So we replaced everything."

I stepped forward, "What?" I was so tired, the words were not making sense.

He explained, "Yes, the pump and tubing were disconnected. So we replaced the tubing too. We've started him on the lowest dosage of medicine, and we'll go from there. Everything went well, and he looks good. He's up and talking already."

Not knowing what any of this meant yet, my concern went to his spine, was there loss of spinal fluid? Apparently not, if he was up and talking. I was told they would buzz us again when we could see Barton in post-op.

Flabbergasted and still trying to piece together how the pump and its connecting tube could have become detached, and even more curious was the length of time it could have been separated. I rode back down the escalator, out of breath.

I found Stan and Nancy packing their computers away, to tell them the news. Barton's father had the same reaction as I did, "What do you mean the pump was disconnected?"

I also called Catherine to let her know the news, but when Nancy placed the buzzing call button in my hands, I said, "I have to go. They are buzzing me again, but I'll call you later once I know more."

I rushed back upstairs, trying to slow my breath. A nurse in a white uniform came out of the doublewide doors, and called my name. I walked behind her as we made our way through the hospital's long corridors, winding in an endless maze. Finally, we entered the post-op room, where five or six patients were all lying in beds next to each other with monitors and machines beeping.

Amazingly, Barton was wide-awake lying on the gurney. He smiled a big goofy smile, and I knew he would be just fine.

"Did you hear?" he asked.

"Yes," I pulled a swivel chair closer, which slid out from under me at first. I sat next to him, "They said the pump was completely disconnected. Can you believe it?"

"If I could do all that without the medicine, what can I do with it?" Barton's father walked in behind me, and I stood up to greet him.

Looped up by the drugs, Barton cracked several jokes, interrupted by the beeping of his cardiac monitor, whenever the pulse oximeter slipped from his finger.

When the nurse came in, he looked up and said, "My heart is beating real good. You don't have to put it back on."

The nurse smiled, as Barton was obviously feeling quite high from the anesthesia. She tried several times to get the finger monitor to stay on, but Barton kept jerking away.

To appease him, she took the monitor off, and the screen above blinked to zero. Barton tipped his head back. "It's zero, that means I'm dead. I'm dead," he called out in a loud, clear voice.

I rubbed the back of his hand, "Barton, hush, sweetie, hush."

The nurse shuffled back over to us, drawing the curtains around us, creating a cocoon. I laughed at how she mumbled something about us being too loud.

After about twenty minutes, Barton's eyes fell shut, and he drifted off to sleep. I sat rubbing between his thumb and forefinger. I looked at his face and noticed his long eyelashes, the high check bones, and silver strands of hair among the thick dark shafts. I noticed the small mole on the tip of his right ear, the smooth skin on his forehead, and his bushy eyebrows with one exceptionally long strand. I rubbed on the finger, where his ring was missing. And his legs, still for the first time since we had ever met.

For several hours, I sat suspended in time, looking at his face and rubbing his hands.

The world buzzed around us. Through a small window behind him, I watched a helicopter take off. A voice crackled overhead. "Message to the ER, prepare for a trauma, ETA five minutes. ER, prepare for incoming trauma."

A man across the room needed to go to the bathroom, but couldn't and was moaning in pain. The elderly woman beside Barton had an unstable heart rhythm. As we sat, Barton passed out on the hospital bed, and I, rubbing his fingers, watched his face.

I didn't have a watch on, but it felt like several hours before the nurse came in to say that a room was ready.

The nurse called out, "Barton, Barton can you wake up for me. I just need to know that you can wake up. Can you wake up?"

Barton shook his head, "No."

We laughed and the nurses took a hold of the edge of the gurney to move him out of post-op. As the attendants moved him across the threshold of the elevator, his eyes popped open. I said quietly, "I'm right here sweetie. They're moving us into a room."

Settled into the hospital room, Barton passed out in the bed, the oxygen tubes still in his nose. I fought with my computer to let our family and friends know the surgery went well. Stan and Nancy found the room shortly after we arrived.

Stan and I stood at the foot of the bed and gazed at Barton's legs, completely still.

We glanced at each other, Stan's face mimicking mine—utter disbelief. At first I was alarmed and thought, "What did they do to him?"

Stan poked at his legs and knees. "Are they crossed?" he asked.

I put my hands on my face and whispered, "I've never seen him so still. Never."

I was thankful to have Stan and Nancy at the hospital, as they made sure I ate something for dinner. Dropping me off at the hospital, I stayed overnight, bringing an overnight bag with a change of clothes and blanket.

All night, Barton woke in fits and starts almost every hour. His body jerked up from the hospital bed, eyes popping open. I stood up so he could see me, "I'm right here, sweetie. I'm right here."

Quickly, he drifted back off.

The anesthesia made Barton's stomach sick and nausea washed over him several times. His blood pressure was low, but he had been asleep for over nine hours. Every hour or two the nurses brought in a physiological monitor to take his vitals.

After 2 am, I twisted and turned to find an agreeable position in a horribly uncomfortable chair that folded like an accordion and is meant for someone much bigger than I. Every time I got one side to lie flat, the other would spring up; I felt like I was teetering on a see-saw.

Our thick Pendleton blanket from home hung over the sides, tucked under my feet. As I turned from side to side, the ring swayed back and forth, the clasp of the necklace catching under my neck from the ring's weight.

An hour later, the nurse came in. "Has he gone to the bathroom at all?" I shook my head.

The nurse spoke to Barton in a high-pitched voice, "If you don't pee in the hour, I'm going to have to put a catheter in. You don't want that do, you? We can't let you go home until we know all your functions are back to normal."

Under normal circumstances, time limits made Barton freeze in panic, especially when it comes to using the bathroom. He protested, "No, I can go, just give me a chance."

The nurse shot a look at him, "Okay, but if you haven't gone by the time I get back, I'm going to have to cath you."

Wide-awake and determined to avoid the alternative, Barton wouldn't go back to sleep until he had gone to the bathroom. I held the urine bottle between his legs, thinking of every joke I could come up with to make him laugh and relax.

Thirty minutes later the dam broke forth, a flood filling the urine bottle to the brim, over a liter of pee. I sloshed the container on the counter to prove to the nurse Barton was indeed functioning normally. With the nurse appeased and Barton comfortable, I returned to the unruly foldout chair.

I had just closed my eyes when the saline drip machine began beeping like a car alarm that would not turn off. After seven times of calling the nurse back into the room to fix the machine, she ordered a new one. By 4 am, I was crashed out on the chair and Barton was now babbling to himself. I caught phrases, half sentences that lay in the air between us.

The next morning, I woke up to the rising sun outside the window, which was quickly crowded out by rain clouds. I changed clothes in the tiny bathroom just in time, because as soon as I walked out, the doctor poked his head in the doorway, making his rounds. Stan and Nancy also arrived to relieve me so I could get some food. After breakfast, Barton's father went down the hall to get a cup of coffee.

"Can I have my ring back on?"

I slipped the ring off the tiny silver chain, and back around Barton's finger, where it belonged.

Even now, there are times when I look at my hand and see my engagement diamond glittering colors of the rainbow, aligned with the cross on my wedding ring. I twist it around my finger when I am nervous.

I treasure our rings that were handmade, and acknowledged the responsibilities of how for a time, I wore the weight of my husband's ring, before slipping it back onto his hand.

He picked at the eggs for breakfast, not ready for a huge meal, but was awake and making some sense. The doctors visited him again, discussing the disconnected pump.

By the afternoon, they pulled the IV drip out and released Barton to go home. Stan and Nancy stayed with Barton as the nurses filled out discharge papers, and I left to go find the car. The rain had finally stopped, and the sun peeked out between gray clouds. Indeed, it was a great day to be going home, where the real work of recovery would begin.

At home, Barton slept off the pain medication. Our black lab, Bear, whimpered at the bottom of the bed. I let Bear up on the bed to be closer to Barton, and Bear curled up at Barton's feet.

I crawled under the covers, too. Barton and I began to talk about the surgery, and process what we had learned.

When I met Barton, the dosage of his medication in his Baclofen Pump was extremely high. In fact, during his first appointment at the Medical Center in Birmingham, they mentioned that they had never seen a dosage so high. We sat in the doctor's office as the doctors tried to calculate the unit of medication and rate to be able to bring the dosage down. During the year we lived in Alabama, the doctors did regulate the dosage to a more manageable level, but Barton seemed not to notice a difference one way or the other.

To me, it didn't mean anything since I had not been with Barton when it was first implanted. We've had many conversations about withdrawal, malfunctions, and reactions.

Barton

Where do science and spirit merge? This was the question we began to ask over Christmas.

When I awoke from the operation table to hear from my doctor that in fact the pump and tube that delivered the medicine were never connected, I found myself in the midst of an identity crisis.

Indeed, I had come face to face with the fact that my spirit, along with my love and connection to God overcame all the physical reasons that had become limiting to my body over the first years of my life.

Honestly, I did not know how to handle this. I did my best to hide my internal struggle, telling Megan, "Yes indeed, I was amazed by this."

Of course I was; something within me was not willing to face the fact that all these efforts in spiritual training were sufficient to overcome such obstacles. I had indeed made a direct connection to God and was discovering new aspects about my belief that I am a whole person.

Ironically, I had written articles about the subject. How clearing out the tangles within our non-physical selves opens the doorway to greater flow and connectivity between the divine and our physical existence, increasing our capacity both physically and spiritually. How, in some ways we are a woven basket for God's love and when these fibers are straight and clear, the connection to the physical becomes interwoven to the point where a person's physical health can affect his spiritual health and vice versa.

My Western education instilled in me the belief in the benefit I was receiving from the medicine only. Having now realized the physical transformation I had been through over the previous years was purely brought on by my explorations into the spirit, the question begged at my soul: How much further could I go since the medicine and pump were operating properly?

In the days and weeks after my surgery, I began to probe where I understood the boundaries between spirit and biology to be and found myself overwhelmed by my discoveries.

I had spent my life breaking through culturally ingrained beliefs of identifying my disability as the core element of who I am. And with it, the assumption I should accept my situation of being confined to a wheelchair rather than stretch beyond my comfort zone and attempt what others considered impossible.

When I was young, I resigned myself to this belief; understanding that life from a wheelchair had its advantages. I could cut to the front of the line at the amusement park. I always had the best parking spot, and I was never at a loss to find the help I needed. I recognized that much of my ability to find the help I needed was due to my personal gumption, but it also rested upon the good nature of those I asked.

I grew up knowing all of the medical reasons why walking was never scientifically possible for someone with such severe Cerebral Palsy, and therefore should never be a personal goal.

As I began to train in martial arts, my perception began to expand. Through meditation, I could relax my muscles and move them in specific ways. There was more than just the physical body, and when I stood up for the first time, I felt the freedom of stretching my body and spirit in unison.

I grew up knowing the medical reasons why walking was never a possibility for someone with severe Cerebral Palsy. So when it was explained to me that I would have to walk if I were to finish my training program as an apprentice healer, I had to make a choice. I could limit myself through fear or move through it, believing I was being supported by the medicine my pump was delivering.

I assumed the medicine from the Baclofen pump was making it easier for me to stand, but since I wasn't receiving the medicine properly, I could no longer hold onto this belief.

I looked at my assumptions about how I had been able to stand, and even walk, during our wedding. Now I was forced to uncover and face the buried belief that I could not have possibly stood on my own, not without Western medicine. But I had.

Whether others recognized it or not, this overwhelmed me for I knew somewhere deep within, I could do more than I ever thought possible, especially now that I was receiving medicine as it was intended. How much more was possible? I had already gone infinitely further than I could have imagined by standing and walking.

My human mind could not fathom anything greater. I didn't want to accept that my standing and walking was out of pure spirit or that I could have walked on my own. I began to doubt everything around me. I knew there was a realm of unknown possibilities I could touch but was unwilling to face because of the doubt that now made its way into my consciousness.

Our heads were spinning. How often do we limit ourselves, create barriers and boxes that prevent us from reaching beyond what we think and assume? If we take away those barriers, how much further can we actually go? Clearly, we were both reeling in these new discoveries of self-limitations and breaking beyond these invisible boundaries.

We were overjoyed at how Barton had made it through major surgery with apparently little pain. Delighted to be home, we were both determined to celebrate Christmas. We ventured out to the Christmas Eve service at the Episcopal Church downtown with gratitude for life and recovery.

During the service, we held hands, gave each other love looks, and I felt the ring around Barton's finger. One time, Barton commented about how I play with my ring, twisting it around my finger, how it resembled prayers during the rosary, moving from bead to bead with each finger.

We experienced a heightened sense of purpose and being alive, in connection with each other, and the inter-connectedness of the physical and spiritual. We relished in the scent of evergreens that wrapped banisters, lighted candles throughout the sanctuary, and incense lingering in the air.

We returned home, only for Barton to crawl back into bed for several days having overdone it. I was brought back down to the realities of after-surgery challenges; making sure Barton had what he needed to recover, getting caught up on missed work, and taking care of the house.

Christmas morning, I was determined to get into the spirit. Barton was still quite sick from the effects of the anesthesia, but I was resolved to feel the Christmas spirit and found myself in the kitchen making praline pecans.

Using a recipe from a friend, I pulled out a blue plastic bowl that I had used many times before with this same recipe. Mixing butter and brown sugar together, I warmed the sweet concoction in the microwave for eleven minutes exactly.

In the midst of baking goodies, Barton's help had arrived, and even though Barton was still feeling sick, he needed a shower. I explained to his help specific instructions on how to help Barton with a shower and to get dressed before returning to the kitchen.

When I opened the door to the microwave, I pulled the bowl up, shocked because it seemed so light. I held the rim of the bowl and watched as the contents slipped down, overflowing in the microwave.

I did a double take.

The boiling praline pecan mix dripped out of the microwave, onto the stovetop below, down the white oven door and onto the tile kitchen floor. This was my Christmas morning.

Barton was in the bathroom, apparently throwing up, when my voice, full of disgust, filtered through the house. I raced to find paper towels, rags, anything that would wipe up the sugary molasses gel. Once it cooled and hardened, I experimented with tools to scrape the brittle off the bottom of the microwave, stovetop cover and the top of our ceramic tile floor. I spent hours cleaning up the congealed concoction that was supposed to be given to family and friends as gifts. Even through my fatigue, I smiled. I had to be strong for Barton's recovery.

Somewhere in the middle of the after-surgery chaos, Christmas cards were written in January, though not mailed until February; I felt like a horrible wife for not having it all together.

Somehow we survived.

Morning Walks on the Beach

Walking beside
crashing waves,
we move, dancing
to the rhythmic flow
of the waves.
Two birds swirling
over the water
into the sun
as it rises over the horizon.
A rainbow rises
into the sky
glistening, connecting
water and earth to heaven.
Our souls meet,
touching deeper
like the vibrant hues
rising to the sun.

With all my love,
Megan

~ Megan M. Cutter. 2003

Chapter Nine

The Talk of Women

Iturned pages of my wedding book, rubbed swatches of fabric and visualized how a flower bouquet would look in my hands. I couldn't help but miss my mother. I had always thought she would be there, on my wedding day. As I considered the wording for our wedding invitations, memories of my mother filled my mind.

In the year before her death, she had been a part of some of the wedding planning for an engagement, which ended in heartbreak.

"Don't you want a big wedding? Your wedding will be the talk of the town. You, my dear, will look like a princess," she would say.

Although, when I found out she had already chosen the bridesmaids dresses, I was furious. "Mom, I can't believe you did that. I can't believe you. They are ugly. I don't want those in my wedding. No way."

At the time, I dismissed her overprotective and pushy advice, so why now, did I miss her unrestrained proposals so much?

Our relationship had been close, and like all mother and daughter relationships, complicated as well. As a child, I would start a fight in the car on the way to school, just so I didn't have to get out of the car to leave her, as I switched houses nearly every day.

I did inherit my mother's creativity, and while mine expressed itself through the written word, I would always admire my mother's paintings and her ability to teach others through creativity.

I knew my mother had Multiple Sclerosis, and from a very early age, I would would rub her legs when she was tired or write cards to cheer her up if she was having a day when she was in pain. While she never used a wheelchair, she did use a cane; one that she embellished with a decoupage of white cats, bearing resemblance to our cat Allie.

Even though her health deteriorated, I always thought she would be there when I was married. Returning to her home after college, I realized that while the Multiple Sclerosis affected her energy level, she led an active life and became a locally known artist and helped others with Multiple Sclerosis lead active lives.

My mother passed away unexpectedly from "complications of Multiple Sclerosis," and what I believe was a reaction to a medication, which was recalled by the FDA multiple times in the years after.

I would spend many nights sifting through papers, often re-reading her letters and notes she had written to me over the years.

One morning, I found a letter she had drafted to a magazine describing my wedding dress in such detail, the fantasy of a southern-belle princess emerging from the movies. In a fit of rage, I ripped it up into tiny pieces and burned it, believing at the time, I had lost everything I had loved.

As I moved through these processes of grief, I would burn some of these writings as a way to let them go, feeling myself reborn, emerging raw and reborn into a new life, and at other times, I would collect her letters, stashing them in a box for when I needed to hear her voice.

I always knew that my mother would have loved Barton. Even though my mother could be a busybody at times, she had a sense of humor that Barton would have played off of with perfect syncopation.

I could hear their laughter echoing and overlapping in my imagination; they would have no doubt laughed and joked, at my expense of course.

While our families were struggling to accept our engagement to someone that none of them knew, I could imagine my mother accepting Barton with open arms, negating all of the resistance we felt from others.

After Barton proposed, I called up an old school friend, Emily. When I described Barton, I could feel Emily's skepticism over the phone lines.

"Are you sure, you're not just trying to take care of someone, since your mother died?" I could hear the condescending tone in her voice.

"Oh, no. Barton and I love each other. This has nothing to do with my mother."

Yes, my mother did have a disability, but did that mean I wanted to marry Barton because he had a disability, too? I loved Barton because he trained in martial arts, because he was a writer, and for his smile and the glint in his bright sky blue eyes. I loved him because he was stubborn, and the mischievous look couldn't be concealed.

Being with my mother did allow for me to see disability in a different light, to be flexible with another's needs, and to be open to doing things differently from taking more time to get from place to place to creative problem solving, thinking nothing of it.

In this respect, I do believe that having a parent with a disability allowed me to be open to Barton in ways that others may not. My mother was just like any other parent, working hard to provide for me in the best ways she knew how, and unconsciously, this gave me a perspective that no matter what a person's ability, their principles and values mattered more than outward appearance.

Still, I distrusted the medical community, furious at the doctor's who approved the medication my mother took the day before she passed away, and experienced anxiety attacks over taking any medication, fearful of undisclosed reactions, that I might die as she did. How fascinating then that I would marry Barton, someone who relied on the medical community to improve his quality of life. Over the years, I would work through my distrust and anxiety about the medical community, in a slow and intense process of healing.

As Barton and I prepared for our wedding, the times when I missed my mother popped up at the most unexpected times: wedding announcements, a wedding shower, trying my dress on or shopping for accessories; these items were sacred for mothers and daughters.

During the wedding ceremony, there was a candle lit in honor of my mother, and while it was never spoken, it was a reminder that her presence was felt.

In many ways, the relationship with my stepmother, Linda, has grown slowly over the years. Sadly, I pushed Linda away as a child, lamenting over the split between parents.

"I have a mother," my rebellious voice would resound.

The relationship would recover from my defiant remarks, but not enough to invite feminine mentorship to flourish through my teen years. While Linda tried in many ways to become closer, I kept her at fingers-tip distance, worried that I would upset my mother if we got too close.

I would share pieces of myself with each side of my family, pieces I thought they would approve of, but unable to share all of who I was with either, fearful of rejection.

Even after my mother's passing, there were certain things I just did not share with my father's side of the family.

The time period during our move to Raleigh was extremely stressful for Barton and me. Not only were we both reeling from the effects of Katrina and picking up and moving on such short notice, we had little support to rely on. I had asked my father if we could borrow their SUV to move, but I didn't know they were in the middle of organizing a conference.

When I arrived in Atlanta to switch cars, I realized that they both had forgotten, and I had to track down the car. Sleep deprived, emotionally exhausted and overwhelmed, I snapped in the parking lot, "I have to get to Raleigh tonight. Where is dad? I can't believe you forgot."

Two weeks later, when I returned their van, I would apologize, but it did little to repair the rift in the relationship.

Only recently have I begun to show pieces of myself that I would keep tucked inside, hidden and apart from what my family would know. I began to share our struggles as well as our successes. Opening dialogue about finances, which was a red button topic, I found a sense of listening and support instead of the criticism I had anticipated.

In the beginning, the transformation was a slow process, and I tested my family's view of Barton and me, and I made leaps into the unknown with jobs and life choices, not always with a soft cushion underneath to catch us if we fell.

Still, my father and Linda began to see us in new ways, and in turn, we also showed more pieces of ourselves. I let go of hiding my vulnerabilities, my family respected those places, supporting us in ways we could not have expected.

One of the most intimate times when Barton and I felt my family's support was when we were in Atlanta for the weekend, and miles away at home, we had to put our puppy to sleep. While we were away, we found out he was not digesting food because his intestines had not developed properly. Barton had a coaching workshop, and I was the one who was on the phone with the emergency vet discussing our options. There was simply nothing we could do.

I waited until Barton was finished with his day of training before we called the vet together. We emerged from the bedroom after making the final decision. Neither Barton nor I could help the tears streaming down our faces, and my dad and Linda came over and both gave us a hug. In that moment, we felt such a profound sense of support.

Coming back to visit my dad and Linda, we have felt a stronger sense of encouragement with discussions over dinner on the back porch, sharing adventure stories and pictures, and conversations over different aspects of our work.

Recently, Linda came to Raleigh with a friend, and we were able to connect for a brunch at one of our favorite restaurants downtown.

Barton shared, "Megan started a new job, and I am just so proud of her. She's grown so much."

Linda smiled, "That's wonderful, Megan. What's it been like for you?"

I answered, "I'm still learning, so it still all feels very new to me. But I love what I'm doing."

We had a delightful conversation over crêpes, homemade French toast and omelets. I also found how much I enjoyed Linda's insights and perspective as we talked. These experiences have given a sense of connection that I would have never expected, and am ever grateful for.

At first, I found myself awkward and unsure of how to relate to anyone in Barton's family, and even in my own because I had had such a profound and complex relationship with my mother.

Looking for acceptance, I was shy at showing the creative and quirky sides to my personality. There were times when I was afraid of what family might think of me if they knew the real me. It took time for me to open up, show my creative personality, and even to talk about our challenges as well as our successes. I wanted my family to think I had it all together; I could do it all, and in the end, I kept pieces of myself hidden away. I was sensitive to what family members thought, how they saw me or if I was doing things right. I had not yet learned to value my own perspective as much as I valued other opinions, especially from other family members.

Over the first few years of our marriage, I felt Nancy's support in little but tangible ways, helping out with airplane fare to New Hampshire, conversations about how we could sustain ourselves, and helping us with an unexpected expense here and there. I could feel her quiet presence in the background, but I was still timid and formal, unsure of how to show my vulnerabilities.

During family gatherings when Barton and I were off doing different things, Nancy and I would talk about different aspects of our relationship and how I was taking care of myself, with small pieces of advice to support me.

When we were out, I felt included in all of their family events. For example, when we visited Chicago for Barton's brother, Andrew's wedding, Nancy took me in to get my hair done by a professional stylist. While Barton was out touring Chicago with the wedding party, I spent the afternoon with cousins. That evening, Barton and I danced during the reception, wheeling across the dance floor, and I felt elegant as we swayed to the music.

Nancy would call me every so often to check on us, ask how we were, what was going on in our lives. Originally, I thought it was because it was easier to speak to me on the phone than Barton, and that she would be able to hear more of the details of our work and life.

"Hi Megan, how are you?"

"Great. Nancy, how are you?"

"We're doing well. I thought I would call to see how you are doing."

"Things are busy, but they are going. Work is going well. We're changing contracts, but there's always more than one iron in the fire. Barton is loving his job, and we're doing really well."

Nancy laughed, "I think you will always be busy, and always have lots going on. It is a challenge to balance contracts, but it sounds like you're learning."

"We are. It is a challenge. I feel very overwhelmed at times, but we're just thankful there is a lot going on."

When we hung up, I realized while I had initiated information about how Barton was doing, she was calling to talk to me. Never once did she even ask about Barton. This was a huge epiphany that left me feeling elated.

One Christmas holiday after we went through many of our challenges that we faced as a couple that included finances and discussion about having children, Stan and Nancy came over to our house. We joined our friends and family from our training group for a great Christmas Day meal.

We laughed at the kids and dogs running around, enjoyed lively discussions and conversations. As I sat across from Stan and Nancy, I realized how special it was to be sharing this part of our life with them, how our family and friends welcomed each other.

During the weekend, we were in the kitchen and Nancy spoke to us, "I'm just so proud of you two. I'm just amazed at how much you two have grown together, and it's amazing to watch."

We all sat in the kitchen for a moment in quiet reflection.

Not all relationships with family members have grown in the same way, and on both on Barton side and on my own, there are places where there is more work to be done, to work out misunderstandings, to show our true selves without feeling judged or rejected, to be heard and come to a place of standing in one's own point of view while respecting the other.

Maybe the maternal role of my mother would never look like the ideal I had pictured in my head, but it has been there—if I open my eyes to see it.

Fertilization

Nibbling a cup,
hummingbird vacillates
before lemon dust
like a cat's whiskers
approximating distance.

Your skin puckers around a breath.
The salt of anticipation crystallizing
nipples as dew beads
gasping relief.

Wings palpate air,
messaging you, while
honey drips into soil.

~ S. Barton Cutter, March 2004

Chapter Ten

Wheelchairs Are Not Made for Sex

Let's get something straight. *Wheelchairs are not made for sex.*
Everyone thinks that Barton's old wheelchair met its end from old age and wear and tear. On the contrary, his former wheelchair bit the dust because of good old-fashioned fun.

Here's the main problem: metal can break and wheelchairs are destructible. It's a fact. It will happen, not a matter of "if," but "when." Barton could be walking home or having lunch, but most of the time, without fail, it's while we're making love. Let me give you some advice—horizontal, not vertical. Be careful if the wheelchair leans back, you don't want to flip over either.

We were in the living room when the first episode happened. I wrapped my legs around the frame and used the back wheel as support for my body weight. Barton provided most of the perpetual motion by thrusting his hips forward or up and down. He pushed down on the footrests and the bolt that holds the two footrests together broke. Barton jolted down a few inches; a shock to both of us, and we heard the sound of metal clanking on the floor.

"Oh shit," he muttered, "Oh well." We finished our passionate love scene, careful not to slide out onto the floor.

Later, we wrapped silver duct tape around the foot pedals, as if we were wrapping a bandage after surgery. Just one of many passionate war wounds to come.

The first time Barton and I were together intimately, I didn't feel uncomfortable or apprehensive at all. I don't know why. It could have been that we emailed poetry back and forth to each other or that we spent hours on the phone. We would joke many times about Neal, who I know only survived those months with earplugs. And I wish that accessible speaker phones were adapted to more intimate moments, but no, it will be seared in my mind the evening Barton's father was visiting him and walked in on a rather private phone conversation, which was apparently out loud for everyone within ear shot to enjoy.

While Barton and I were known to have lengthy conversations on the phone and swap insatiable love poems lapping in sexual connotations, I was a little nervous the first time I flew out to Tucson. However, when I found myself in his arms, there was little question about the intimacy that unfolded between us. Our closeness wrapped around the way we looked at each other, our comments or movements such as the sweep of Barton's hand on my leg. Later, we swapped a piece of chocolate through our lips.

I found out quickly I had to watch how I helped Barton with meals when one of my friends teased me at a night out eating pizza. Apparently, I was being a little too flirtatious in how I was maneuvering food into Barton's mouth. I learned quickly that our more intimate trifles should remain out of the public arena.

Our first time together in Tucson, we never made it to the bedroom. Instead, his wheelchair provided the perfect angle, or so we thought. Thank God I am flexible. The arm frame is clunky and has gears and joints that always stick out. Figuring out where my legs should rest without being impaled by pieces of metal is always a challenge.

Afterwards, I had an imprint of a piece of metal running along the inside of my thigh. One time, I impaled my toe on the wheel. That was not pretty, especially when we were focused on other things.

Another time, I had my leg hung over the side, and while I didn't think I was pushing that hard, we both almost lost balance as the side of the wheelchair suddenly lowered by about six inches. We had broken an armrest and two pieces of metal soldered onto the frame. Now come on; we weren't being that rough.

One afternoon, I mentioned to Barton, "We should call the manufacturers and offer to test "drive" their up and coming models."

Cackling, he replied, "I don't think they'll find it as amusing as we do."

I have the amazing ability to let my mouth just say what I am thinking, sometimes without restraint. One night we were having dinner with friends and one of them made a comment about the shocks on Barton's new wheelchair, as it had great springs, rocking back and forth.

"I know. They're much better than the old ones." I stood on the back, and lightly pushed up and down, rocking the wheelchair. You get the drift, right?

Our friend turned away sticking his fingers in his ears, "I don't want to know. I don't want to know. Too much information!"

We don't mean to, but apparently we shock more people than we know by little comments like this one. What can I say—insert foot into mouth. (or in my case, "change feet").

I did have to get over the embarrassment of Barton's direct support staff when we were in Tucson when the next morning Barton's help walked right in. I was in rare form so early in the morning, but jumped up and made a beeline for the bathroom. I put my head in my hands and shook my head; it was pretty obvious we had had some fun the night before. I stood in the bathroom for at least half an hour, not knowing what to do with myself.

There have been times when I've wondered what his assistants that help him get dressed in the morning must think of us, when it's pretty obvious what we've been doing the night before.

We will always be playing with new positions and how to get from here to there. But of course, experimenting is a challenge when you are dealing with a wheelchair, so be careful.

One more piece of advice, don't forget where you are. If you made love in bed, you are in bed, and it is a fairly private place. You can have sex in a wheelchair anywhere, but don't forget where you are. Once, during our first weekend of being together, we left the window blinds open and a poor friend's mother was shocked and is still recovering from our passionate lovemaking scene in the living room. Any other incidents such as this one—we'd rather not know that anyone else has caught us in the act.

After Barton got his newest wheelchair, of course we had to break it in right away. On this one, we could raise the arms, and lift the foot pedals, too. With the press of a button, it reclines back, which makes the weight much easier on me. Though, we realized it would be nice if his wheelchair lasted another year, so we found other places for our fun.

As for the, "How do we, well, you know?" We do it like any other couple. Do you really need us to be that detailed? Barton has muscle spasms, which can be both detrimental and pleasurable. We were on vacation and having a little fun in bed when I was on top of him, and his arm locked out in front of his stomach. I nearly went rolling off the bed, at the just most impeccable moment. The positives—muscle spasms, oh muscle spasms. Need I say more? Really?

After Barton's surgery, we had many questions about how the medication would affect Barton's body mechanics. There was a while where he had some interesting reactions. Still, we had to approach each other with curiosity and playfulness, learning the new language of our bodies together.

We find that we constantly have to renew our intimate lives. It's so easy to let the long list of things to do, working, logistics, the conversations and discussions, to all get in the way. When we continue to reconnect, we play with positions that, whew, amp up our fun in the bedroom.

Intimacy is not just about sex.

Our time together changes over the years, and we figure out how to connect on different levels with a sense of playfulness. However—our sex life is often a curiosity for others.

After I came home sporting an engagement ring, I was unprepared for the barrage of questions I would receive about our intimate lives together.

When we were first engaged, I would beam with excitement, "We met training in martial arts, and we're both writers. He sends me a poem everyday."

When asked in more detail about Barton, I would explain, "Barton has Cerebral Palsy, so he uses a motor and manual wheelchair to get around."

Well, how do you, you know? How can you have children? So are you adopting kids since you can't have your own? How are going to go without sex? You poor thing. Getting married to a disabled guy, for shame.

The questions and assumptions were endless. My favorite was from my Episcopalian priest and mentor, "So can I ask, does the plumbing work?"

In my head, I have all kinds of responses to these questions. *How do you have sex? Does your plumbing work? Never mind, you have two kids, you're a priest; I don't want to know. Can you have children?*

There was this overall assumption that I would never again have sex in my life, which is completely untrue. Instead of snapping some rank retort, I keep my mouth shut, and smile because I really don't think anyone means harm.

I pause, giving someone a few minutes to wrap their brain around a courteous and polite response, leaving out all the juicy details; there are plenty of juicy details.

I never thought I would become a sex education teacher. We haven't written a sex manual, but I'm sure it's not too far off. When we speak at conferences around the country, as long as the audience is old enough or with respectful and tasteful language, we welcome the opportunity to break some earth shattering myths.

There's an assumption that people with disabilities don't get married, don't hold a job, can't have sex, can't have children.

Sex and disabilities in the same sentence. We are so open about intimacy because in many areas, it's still such a taboo subject. Direct support staff may not know how to assist their clients in creating healthy relationships, and agencies or group homes may not want to become liable for the many issues intimacy can bring with it. Even families may not know how to cope with their children's development or what language may be appropriate for someone with an intellectual or developmental disability.

With so many debates on intimacy publically, religiously and within the family realm, this discussion blossoming in the disability community only heightens the intensity of views and perspectives.

Still, many youth and adults with disabilities, families, and advocates have questions but don't know who they can ask or where they can turn to find the answers. In many cases, there is no one clear answer but rather an ongoing conversation, education and dialogue.

When Barton and I met, we were in our early/mid twenties, and we were in love. We didn't have huge discussions over intimacy beforehand, it happened naturally, as with any young adults in love.

Being with Barton for the first time broke down all my own expectations about how someone in a wheelchair could love in an intimately healthy way. Over the years, we have found many couples, advocates, and families who do have questions, and I have had to get over blushing faces and whispered answers.

We share our story openly, not to shock but to open the dialogue of intimacy, for all people of all abilities.

A family first must decide on their own beliefs and their own teachings. We also know there are many situations and other factors such as group homes, institutions, families or direct support staff that affect how a young adult cultivates relationships with others.

How do you create a healthy relationship? What is appropriate behavior in public, in private? What do you do when someone touches you inappropriately? How do you know if you've been abused? What are qualities of a boyfriend or girlfriend who make a good match? These are questions we all should discuss.

Many people see me riding in Barton's lap around town, especially when he wants to take me on a dinner date. We're used to the looks from others inside their cars.

We look at each other. "Did you see their face? That was complete shock."

"The girl was grinning at us, though."

Some people smile, while others gawk. We don't care.

One summer day, we were waiting outside at a restaurant. I was sitting in Barton's lap, and he started doing 360-spins on the sidewalk. I laughed and screamed with delight, which caused many heads to turn.

For those who recognize it, I don't have to be sitting on Barton's lap for our connection to shine through. One Valentine's Day after five years of marriage, we ventured over to a local restaurant for a special treat.

We didn't know it, but behind us a couple had been watching as we swooned over each other. When the couple got up to leave, the wife stopped by our table. She slid a vase with two red roses onto our table, "It is my husband's birthday today, and we just couldn't help but notice the love between you. We hope you enjoy."

The rest of the evening, we cherished the roses and began looking at other couples in the restaurant. Can you see love? How do you know? Over in the corner, a woman hid behind her menu, and the man seemed really into her, but it was clear she didn't feel the same way. We looked again and watched several couples who seemed to be delighted in each other's presence.

Then, we saw two older couples sitting together. They must have been in their seventies or eighties. As we left, we asked, "Are you celebrating this Valentine's Day?"

"Yes, it's our anniversary," one of the women said, "But we decided to go out on a double date."

"Someone gave us these roses, and we wanted to pass them along to you," I put the vase of roses on the table. We smiled at them as we left the restaurant.

When we walked outside, snow was still falling. I hopped on Barton's lap, and he drove us down white-dusted roads. Soon our heads were covered with white flakes. I teased Barton about his white eyebrows. He just zoomed faster into 360-spins in the road. The evening was magic. We were in a winter wonderland, with just the two of us out on the roads. Barton making wheelchair tracks in the snow, and me screaming in delight as he whipped me around in circles.

Other times though, sitting in Barton's lap has made other people around us uncomfortable. Once, we were having lunch with a close friend, Betty, and as we were waiting, I slid into Barton's lap. We could tell Betty was uncomfortable as she tried to convince me to sit in the empty seat next to her. It was clear that our intimate behavior bothered her. This surprised both Barton and me to some extent as she was someone who knew us well.

When people look at us as a couple, there is a natural assumption that I provide for all of Barton's needs, and it's hard to explain how Barton gives me what I need, physically, emotionally and intimately. Sometimes, it doesn't matter how well we try to explain, but in the end, it doesn't matter.

By far, the most exciting and adventurous aspect of our relationship has been exploring our intimacy, provided we don't break Barton's wheelchair into smithereens first.

Love

When it spins out
into the web
like a pine tree
mounted against darkness,
the raindrop erupts
ocean-like into this moment,
Creation is reborn.

Egoless, the river pours through
baskets of gold pollen;
Baptism of the spirit!
And then another breath.

~ S. Barton Cutter, February 26, 2003

Chapter Eleven

Who Is He To You?

The alarm went off at 5:30 am, rolling onto my back I noticed a soft light coming from our office across the hall. As I gained consciousness, I noted the rhythmic tapping of Megan's fingers across her computer keyboard.

"God knows how long she's been awake," I thought, "I'd better get going, too, before I'm late."

As the thought lingered in my mind, Megan rushed in, grabbed my bath chair, tore the covers off and had me seated on the edge of the bed before I knew what was happening.

"I was looking at the bank account, and we have five bucks left. Oh, and by the way, I finished writing my article. I was wondering what you wanted me to do with the car tomorrow."

"Uh, huh," I grumbled.

"All right, let me get you a shower because I know you need to get going. I have to meet Becky at ten and then Adriana at two, and then I need to run by the bank and the post office. And then I need to pick up Heartworm medicine for the dogs, but I need to know what credit card to use. And after that, I need to pick up ink."

"Uh, huh." For the past six months, Megan had been getting up regularly at three am to get work done. Three years into our marriage, I had just started a new job and Megan was working all hours to fill in the gaps that my seven months of unemployment had left, including not having a direct support staff to help me in the mornings. By the time she got me up most mornings, her mind was already racing, and I struggled to process even one of her questions to give a reasonable response.

After I showered and shaved, Megan and I were in the bedroom selecting my clothes for the day when I glanced over at my wheelchair.

"That's odd," I thought, "Megan must have unplugged it before getting me up or maybe when I was in the shower."

"Love, you did plug my wheelchair battery in last night, didn't you?" I said aloud.

"Oh crap, you didn't remind me," She began pacing back and forth, "What if I plug it in now?"

"That won't give me enough charge. I need to go at least eight miles today."

"Well, I'll just move my meeting. What if I took you? I could take you. We'll just take your manual chair, and I'll take you. Let me call to cancel my meeting."

I asked, "Are you sure?"

"Well, what else are you going to do?"

"I don't know. Need to get this partnership established, and if I move the meeting, I'll never get them face to face."

"I'll just take you, then." Megan scowled as she stormed out of the room.

A half an hour later, we were both piling into the car. Megan was so rushed in getting us out the door, I don't actually know if the dogs were fed or if my clothes were on straight.

I knew the general vicinity of where the office building was, and how to get there, at least by bus, but when Megan asked for directions, I gave a fairly accurate guess. However, once we arrived on the office complex, I didn't know where to go. I had planned half an hour of padding when I was traveling alone to wander around and find my way with plenty of time. But now we were late, we were both in sour moods, and there was no time for finding our way.

When we finally located the correct two-story brick building with white trim that reminded me of an early twentieth-century school house, we took a moment in the parking lot to collect ourselves before Megan dropped me off. Once my meeting was over, Megan came in to help me out of the building.

As we left the conference room, Megan and I followed the receptionist into the elevator, and stood against the opposing wall facing her. The meeting had gone well. Those who were there were eager to collaborate, and I was quite relieved that after a long and somewhat frustrating morning, the meeting itself was a breeze. The receptionist was polite, though the expression on her face showed some mild discomfort.

"Where did you find such a good-looking assistant?" A comment meant to break the ice and relieve her curiosity about the dynamic between Megan and me. I was caught off guard. It had been a long time since anyone assumed Megan was my assistant, but realizing the brevity of the elevator ride, I threw out the first response that came to mind, "Because she said yes."

This was probably not the clearest or most appropriate response and in retrospect, I felt a sense of self-betrayal in giving into her assumption that the beautiful woman standing behind me was anyone other than my wife.

The period between my jobs was long, both emotionally and financially. We did our best to conserve our resources, leaving the responsibility of my personal care in the mornings to fall on Megan alone. Clearly, we had allowed this interim period between direct support assistants to drag on far too long.

Two days after my meeting and the incident in the elevator, we fumbled through our day. In an awkward state of irritability, Megan came to me and said, "I don't feel like your wife anymore. I could be anyone. I'm just your help, that's all I am to you."

This was a bad sign. Our focus had shifted from love and mutual respect to pure survival leaving a distorted balance in our relationship. Clearly time for a change. Megan and I began the search for someone who could come in each morning, assist me in the basics of my morning routine.

Up until this point, finding and utilizing support to get me up from bed and going in the morning, I had relied primarily on college students as well as a few brief attempts to use disability providers. In each instance, reliability became a major point of contention. For the college students, the early mornings were a challenging time to show consistency in their schedule. Not realizing the importance of my getting out of bed, they were late, missed days entirely and didn't give advance notice when they had a scheduling conflict. All of this led me to a nagging anxiety, wondering if and how I was going to get out of bed each morning.

My experience with finding a personal care assistant through disability agencies was, by and large, not much better. While these agencies were supposed to have mechanisms built in to account for staff that did not make their shift, rarely were they able to find last-minute replacements to meet my needs.

Before meeting Megan, I always found a way to stumble through these situations, many of which were less than ideal. As a young man living independently, I was at ease with this struggle. Once Megan and I got married, however, having a wife and new responsibilities to our family brought a perspective that I could have never anticipated.

One morning, while we were still living in Alabama, Megan scrambled to get ready for work, and noticing that my direct support person had not arrived yet, I convinced Megan not to worry, and to go ahead and leave, believing that he would arrive within a few minutes. Two and a half hours later, Megan called to see how my morning was going. I answered from bed, "Well, he's not here yet. Can you give him a call?"

"What are you talking about, he's not there yet? Are you freaking kidding me? It's 10:30."

"Just call and see where he is. I'm sure he overslept and once he wakes up, he'll be here."

I laid awake for another hour and a half waiting on him. On her lunch break, Megan rushed home to find me still in bed.

"This is ridiculous. It's noon, and he was supposed to be here five hours ago. You're still in bed. You haven't gone to the bathroom. You haven't had a thing to eat, and I'm sure you had things you needed to take care of this morning. This is not acceptable."

"Yea, it is kind of annoying, but give him a break. He's a college student, and I'm fine, besides being a bit frustrated."

"You're fine. Is that what you call this? Being fine. So it's okay if you never get out of bed? It's okay that you just rot here? You're my husband. This is not fine."

"Okay, I see your point."

From the outside, most people naturally saw Megan as my caretaker. I, however, did everything I could in those early years of our marriage to utilize any help before hers. In this moment, however, I realized my willingness to accept support from those who clearly could not recognize the value of another human's needs were vastly diminishing my own ability to engage in this world as I intended.

As Megan and I were re-entering the search for support, it was clear to both of us the sources I had previously used were no longer acceptable. In addition to my own needs, we also needed someone who could support me in taking better care of Megan, to restore that balance within our relationship.

We decided that we may have more success with someone in the nursing profession, though, unbeknownst to us, this was not quite what I needed either.

Brianna was well qualified and highly recommended. She brought with her a host of experience from working in hospitals and nursing homes in addition to caring for people who are aging. We were excited and grateful to have found someone of her caliber. During the interview, she was confident, to the point, and communicated a strong sense of dedication to being on time and performing well. Nothing seemed out of place.

By the time she began, almost immediately after her interview, Megan and I had done a great deal of self reflection and I began to draw clear distinctions about how I could best support Megan as her husband. Having someone else in the house to assist me in my morning routine would allow Megan the freedom to start taking care of herself again and enough space for each of us to begin moving back into our natural roles of husband and wife.

The first day, however, I came face to face with the realization that using this new support to further a healthy dynamic between Megan and me was not going to happen as easily as I hoped.

After dressing and exercising, it was time for breakfast, and I was excited to have the opportunity to make something for Megan as well. I began down the hall to ask Megan what she would like, and said to Brianna, "I want oatmeal. Let me see if Megan wants any."

Before I could even get out of the kitchen, she replied, "No. I'm here to take care of you. I'm not making her breakfast."

Okay, I thought, this was more or less reasonable as I could see how she might view this as outside of her role. I merely assumed it may take some time for her to warm up to how I operate.

As the weeks went on, both Megan and I began to feel some subtle shifts in our household dynamic, which neither of us had anticipated. When we hired Brianna, we emphasized that Megan may be around most mornings, however questions needed to be handled by me. This was not only because the person we hired was here to assist with what I needed when I got up in the morning, but also because the point behind hiring someone was to allow Megan more time for herself.

Whenever Brianna had a question, she would automatically go to Megan even when I was able to answer. The first few times, I merely assumed she was unable to understand me or she was too impatient to bother. I soon learned this was not the case.

Over and over Brianna assumed my incompetence, and as a result, I noticed a subtle disdain by Brianna to accept any of my direction. I asked her to tie my boots all the way up, and she refused. I have a specific order in which I take a shower and get dressed, and after several days of telling her what I needed and how, she still picked out her own agenda.

In the wake of Brianna's behavior during my morning routine, I continually found myself frustrated by the time her shift was over. As a result, my irritability transferred to Megan as we began our workday. Moreover, Brianna's refusal to accept my guidance forced Megan into a position of having to be on-hand to supervise. In essence, Brianna's view of Megan was as a caregiver, not as a wife.

I remember one morning in particular, Brianna was obsessed for some reason over how I was able to use the bathroom. I explained my normal routine assuming that it was simply part of her curiosity. However, after asking the same questions several times in a row, almost in an attempt to catch me in a presumed lie, my suspicions escalated. After a forty-five minute monologue on when and how I used the bathroom, she seemed satisfied. The next morning as I was mid-way through my exercise routine, Megan happened to stroll through the kitchen where my assistant was waiting for me to finish.

"Does Barton have control over his bowels?" she asked Megan in the same tone with which she questioned me the day before.

"Yes." Megan looked shocked by her question.

"When does he go?"

Megan replied, "He tends to go in the afternoon or evening."

"How often does he pee during the day? Does he have good bladder control?"

"Yes, he's fine." Megan answered in a rush to get back to the project she was working on. I laughed. This was the exact same conversation I had had with Brianna the day before.

While Megan glossed over these questions to get back to work, later on Megan discussed how uncomfortable she felt answering them. Brianna's questions further emphasized the role she saw Megan in, as a caretaker for someone less competent, not a wife in equal partnership with her husband.

I searched for an appropriate opportunity to discuss why I needed Brianna to understand I was fully capable of making decisions and directing the course of my life as an independent adult man. I did not appreciate being treated as anything less.

Fortunately, I did not have to wait long. The next morning I had the perfect opportunity while eating breakfast. "Yesterday, while I was exercising, I noticed that you asked Megan the exact same questions you asked me the day before. Were my answers not sufficient for you?"

"They weren't the same questions," she stammered, "I thought of some other questions. They weren't the same."

They were, though, and it frustrated me even further that she assumed I would not be able to recognize the redundancy. At this point, I chose not to push any further as, from my perspective, it appeared to be a lost cause.

Regardless of her intent, it was clear to me that, at some level, she viewed me as being incapable of providing trustworthy information about my own needs and desires.

The purpose of help in our family is primarily two-fold. The first is to allow me the independence to fulfill my role as a husband, and provide me with the support I need. The second, which is a natural by-product of the first, is to allow Megan the space and freedom to express herself and do what she needs to do, both as an individual and as a wife.

In this particular instance, neither purpose was being fulfilled, nor could they be. When this personal care assistance refused to recognize me as a whole person, it subconsciously transformed our martial [marital] relationship from a husband and wife partnership into a dependency between someone needing care and a person giving it.

Of course, this dynamic merely reinforced the dependence that Megan and I were trying to resolve within our relationship. After an in-depth discussion between the two of us, where we took into careful consideration each aspect of what was going on, we decided it was time for Brianna to move on.

The learning that we took from this experience gave us new insights to consider in the years that followed, as we re-examined our hiring process to reflect more accurately the role that I play as a man and husband, and especially the kinds of support that I need in order to successfully carry this out.

Sustaining the balance of our relationship, and how others perceive our relationship can be just as difficult outside of our home as it is inside.

After we had just moved to Raleigh, we would take the bus to church downtown, so Barton could be in his motor wheelchair. One Sunday morning on our bus ride home, I noticed the bus driver kept looking at us in her rearview mirror. Of course, Barton and I were making faces at each other, typical when we are out and about.

When the driver stopped the bus and began un-strapping the seat-belts that secured Barton's motor wheelchair, she asked me, "Who is he to you? Is he your brother?"

"We're married," I replied.

"What?" She unraveled the seatbelt straps from around Barton's wheelchair and looked at me.

I repeated, "We've been married for two years."

She took a minute to lower the wheelchair lift on the bus, "I could tell you weren't brother and sister. There was something about the way you look at each other."

Clearly she had seen the undeniable presence that crosses between lover's eyes, the unspoken language that takes place in the middle of meetings or lectures, driving down the road, or relaxing at a café down the street.

There is this look, this moment when you can see the assumptions burst. She had seen it, and she got it.

By now, I am quite used to people, who we know or who we don't know, looking at us, trying to figure out how we are related.

I typically respond, "No, I'm not his sister. We're married."

Many on-lookers will also make well-intentioned remarks. "You are such a good woman to have married him."

How do I come back from an off-handed comment? I usually just smile because there is no way to convey the depth of our relationship in such a short amount of time. Why should I have to explain that Barton is a man, my husband, who takes care of me just as much as I take care of him?

I am not Barton's keeper or caretaker. I don't tell him what to do, harp about what he eats or doesn't eat or remind him to be careful when he leaves the house. Yes, there are times when he does need help, but who doesn't?

How can I explain the ways in which Barton supports me, emotionally and even physically? The ways in which Barton knows what our family needs, the times when he runs to pick up dinner because I've had a rough day, how I lie across him as he rubs my back or shoulders, and times when we are intimate. When Barton holds me in his arms, I feel safe and loved.

In most cases, I am never able to express any of these aspects of our marriage in a way that people can tangibly grasp.

I stop myself short, and leave it as, "We're happily married."

There have been times, however, when I have been passionate about advocating not only for our relationship, but to interrupt the perception that because Barton has a disability, he is not capable.

My first experience with this depth of emotion was when the disability organization had told my family I should not marry Barton because it would be too hard for us. While the director may have had good intentions, the mayhem that was left from the concerns of my family hearing the disapproval lingered long after our wedding.

Several years after Barton and I had moved to North Carolina, I reflected on the response of the director, how much it influenced how my family saw Barton, and all of the raw emotions welled up again. Isn't this what disability organizations are for, to advocate all rights for people with disabilities, to live full, healthy lives?

Dear Sir,

I remember like yesterday walking into your office and sitting in the chairs in a conference room with my aunt on one side and you on the other. My fiancé was living in Arizona, and he was moving to Tuscaloosa in May. We were contemplating moving to Birmingham, since Tuscaloosa had so little resources for those living with disabilities. My husband has Cerebral Palsy and uses both a motor and a manual wheelchair.

I remember when you told me not to marry him. That later on in life, it would be hard, and to seriously consider the consequences of marrying someone with a disability. We went over the components of living with someone with a disability. Housing. Transportation. Medical Issues. When I left your office, to be honest, I was floored. I thought you were on my side, and would help my aunt see that marrying someone with a disability was not an impossibility. How could you sit in front of us and tell me not to marry him? You are supposed to be an advocate, supporting those with disabilities.

Instead, I now had to overcome all of the obstacles and stereotypes that you reinforced during that meeting. To this day, I am still seen as an outsider with some of my extended family. Fortunately, while we were engaged, my father was able to see us in an intimate setting dancing at a cousin's wedding reception, which opened his eyes to the love in our relationship. Over the years, he has seen how my life has changed, for the better. He has moved from concern about his daughter to joy about our relationship and life together.

My husband and I married in November of 2004 in Tuscaloosa. My aunt was not able to come because her daughter was giving birth, and I wish she, and you, had been able to attend. Our friends and family saw my husband stand and walk for the first time publically down the aisle. It was a true celebration and yes, a miracle. Every morning, my husband stands and walks, not just for his physical health, but for his family.

Yes, we learned that Tuscaloosa would not provide us

with the services to sustain our lives together. I was miserable at my own job, and my husband wanted more independence and opportunities finding employment. We began searching for a better place, and we had already decided Birmingham would be no better than Tuscaloosa, from my discussion with you and others. Right after Katrina, I quit my full time job and we moved to Raleigh, North Carolina. My husband concentrated on freelance writing contracts while I wrapped things up with the house in Alabama.

My husband and I have been married for two and a half years. We absolutely love Raleigh, where he works to support his family. For a year, he has taught teenagers with disabilities advocacy and empowerment skills, organizing a conference for youth transitioning from high school to college as well as working on additional writing projects. This year, he will be moving into other areas of advocacy programs, and it is clear he offers so much experience to the organizations he will be working with. Together, we have taught self-defense classes to those with and without disabilities. Like any other married couple, we discuss finances, transportation, children, and the future. He takes very seriously his job to protect and provide for our family.

So, why is it that I am writing to you now, after all of this time? Just to let you know that there is love in this world that is so deep and compassionate, and that it can overcome any obstacle. Knowing that while being realistic is important, so is hope and faith.

Since I have met Barton, I have experienced more joy in my life than I have ever thought possible. I have laughed more than I have in my entire life, and am living life, instead of just going through the motions. Before I met him, I had a full time job, little outside responsibility and yes, even engaged to a non-disabled man, who ended up cheating on me. All of that has melted away over these last few years. Yes, marriage takes a lot of work. Neither one of us chose an easy path; we haven't chosen an easy path for much of our lives. Life is hard; it throws curve balls at the most inopportune times. And we move forward through these challenges, together, with so much love.

Maybe the future will be even harder, maybe he will age faster, maybe we will have more medical issues and financial issues to contend with. It is worth it. It so incredibly has been worth it. I am privileged to see the love of God in my husband's eyes everyday. He pushes me, to be a better than I am, everyday. I wouldn't want it any other way.

I hope sharing our story has been helpful. Please pass on our hope to others; it is so incredibly important.

Sincerely,

Megan McLeod Cutter

This would become the first of several family-advocacy letters I would write. Since that time, I have written letters to a national speaking organization who didn't want Barton to become a member because of his slurred speech, to a church whose gate always seemed to be locked, and others. In this case, I received a most touching reply.

Dear Megan:

Thank you very much for your letter. I am so happy for you and Barton. I remember very well our discussion and also seeing The Birmingham News about your wedding. In our discussions I did not feel that I was telling you not to get married, but in retrospect, I am sure I did convey the message. I was not an advocate, and I did not support you or Barton. For that I am profoundly sorry. You are correct, in that I should have portrayed all the possibilities that individuals with disabilities can accomplish . . . exactly what you and Barton have accomplished.

My concern at the time was whether Barton would be able to receive the supports he had received in Arizona. I had talked with a case manager who was trying to assist his move to Alabama, but I was unable to offer any hope that he could receive any services as he had in Arizona. I had also just lost a funding battle with a state agency, in which I was no longer to be able to provide independent living supports to individuals with severe disabilities. However, this is not an excuse for my failure to offer you and Barton support in this important time in your life. I am also sorry that I caused difficulty with your family in their support of your decision.

You and Barton are truly role models for individuals with and without disabilities. If possible, I would like to be able to refer other people to you who are planning for their future. You would be able to offer valuable advice as they pursue their dreams. There are so few husbands and wives who have accomplished what you have. It is very exciting what you are doing in advocacy efforts, and I am glad you have shared it with me.

I would like to request the next time you are in Birmingham, I have the opportunity to apologize to you and Barton personally. I would like to see, as your father has seen, the love that has moved mountains. Thank you for telling me your story, and I hope I have the opportunity to be able to assist you in some small way. You have reminded me why I am in this position to let everyone know why hope is so important in all our lives and how we should share this with everyone. Thank you again for sharing your story. I hope I have the opportunity to talk with you and Barton in the near future.

Sincerely.

This response was an amazing reminder that there are many people who work hard on behalf of people with disabilities who have experienced heartache over losing their own battles, who bring their own perspective from what they have experienced or who may have such a large case load, experienced burn out, fatigue, and many times go unacknowledged in the work they do.

This dialogue created a conversation, a framework of mutual understanding that there are times of frustration and hardship, just as there are times of hope and success. Coming to see both aspects creates a whole and balanced perspective.

Now, when we receive comments and questions about our relationship, I am more open to explaining the ways in which Barton takes care of me, just as the times when I care for Barton. And there are times when we don't feel like explaining it, when we just want to be any normal couple out and about our way.

Still, because we are so active as leaders in our community, we can't help but share our experiences as an inter-ability couple, answering questions and blasting through the assumptions of others defining what this relationship should or should not look like.

We have seen the moment when someone gets it, gets us, realizes that the assumptions that they held about people with disabilities are no longer true. And upon realizing that their perspectives about us were limiting, they are then forced to re-examine the perspective they hold about themselves.

First breath

Wedding blanket
wrapped around our bodies,
skin soft with love's sweat.
We hold her between us,
within our breath;
she pulses until she finds her place,
nestling.
I see her spinning,
dancing in the sunlight.
We are quiet,
lips lightly touch
until we are awakened.

–Megan M. Cutter, 2005

Chapter Twelve

Stork Hunting

Even before we were engaged, Barton and I spent the Tucson afternoons, half-awake, half dreaming about having children. We envisioned a little girl and a little boy, being at a café, bright blue eyes and childhood giggles. We even named them, knowing our family would grow beyond just the two of us.

Like many couples, we waited until we were settled into our apartment in Raleigh before seriously talking about having children. After we began building our writing business, we were sure the time was right.

With a dry mouth and shaking with excitement, I would purchase pregnancy test strips, wondering if this would be the right month. I don't know why I was embarrassed, but I still hid them in the bottom drawer in the bathroom.

I would wonder, "Will it be this month? Please let me be pregnant. Please, God. Please."

Instead, I would find myself in the bathroom a week later, crestfallen at my timely cycle. Timely. A sick feeling would tighten in my stomach, and I would move the pregnancy test strips even further back in the drawer.

Only inside a steamy shower would I let out the tears and sobs that vibrated through my body, wondering what we did wrong. We could feel the connection between us, couldn't we?

I would ask myself over and over, "Is it me? What did I do wrong? I was too stressed, too anxious. We didn't get the timing right. We weren't open enough."

Each month became more stressful, with more unanswered questions, and after a while, it took a daily toll on both of us. This tapped into my old childhood patterns of not believing I was good enough, and I could tell Barton thought something was wrong with him, too.

I couldn't stand the cycle that began and ended each month in disappointment, shame and guilt. We knew we had to take steps to find out what was going on, but neither one of us knew where to begin, and the whole process just embarrassed us. We knew that tests for me might be more invasive, and so we began on Barton's side.

We could take a sample from home to have sperm counted at a reproductive office, which we did. When the test results came back that there weren't any, but the sample could have been contaminated; both of us were embarrassed to do it again. Still, we both had to know. We reluctantly made an appointment with Barton's urologist, the only doctor we knew who would be able to tell us how to find out for sure.

While we waited for hormone tests to come back, we sat in the urologist's office, white and bare except for a table and two chairs. We held hands, tightly interlacing our fingers. We didn't talk or even look at each other. We both were holding our breath. Whatever the results were, we could handle it, right?

The doctor came back and looked at Barton, "You're testosterone is really high, you're defiantly a guy. However, there's this other hormone that you need to produce sperm, and it's really low. So, you aren't making any sperm."

Barton asked, "Is it because of my CP? And if not, will it ever change?"

"No, it isn't. What I'm telling you, I've told hundreds of other men.

But, it's not likely to ever change."

Unexpectedly, the tears began streaming down my face; I couldn't stop them. I turned away as the doctor finished his conversation with Barton.

"Take as much time as you need," the doctor said and left us alone in the examination room.

I leaned over, burying my head in Barton's shoulder. We both took a deep breath trying desperately to comprehend the results and grasp how our lives would ever encompass having a child.

Several years later, we would find that we both had varying hormones contributing to infertility; we were a pair made for each other after all. We would never have children, not the natural way anyway.

Our conversations afterward were full of the awkwardness of our questions and the unpredictable journey now ahead of us.

Obviously we had to get back on track with our everyday lives, but we also had to look at the fact that having children naturally was a lost dream that we couldn't change. I would not get pregnant. We would not see a snapshot or ultrasound of a baby in the womb; Barton would never get to put his hands on my belly or listen to a baby's heartbeat.

No one followed up with us about our options for adoption or alternatives to natural conception. In many cases, couples try for years, or there may be issues relating to the woman's hormone balance, which may include more discussion and conversation with professionals.

After the conversation from Barton's urologist, we heard from no one. No one told us about how to even wade through the mounting questions swirling in our heads. How could we create our family?

There was no one to have a conversation with, no one to ask questions of, nothing but a dream—crushed.

I threw away the pregnancy strips, the hormone tracking charts, and we hardly touched each other at night, a numbness which neither one of us could speak to each other about.

When we did have conversations about where to go next or what to do, we were never quite on the same page with the back and forth discussions, questions and ethical concerns that followed.

"I want to have a baby right now, we can do sperm donation. I'll be 35, and it'll be too late."

"You'll be 35 in three years. We have plenty of time," Barton laughed.

I felt dismissed. I pushed harder. "No we don't. What if it takes us time to go through sperm donation? They say there's only a 5 percent chance each month. And what if that doesn't work, then we'll have to adopt no matter what."

"But Megan, we should have the finances in order, and my contract may change in a few months. We should be more stable."

I didn't understand. Many couples who expect naturally aren't stable or perfect. They figure it out as they go along, and they are fine. Anger welled up. Why does someone who isn't ready to have children get to have a baby, and I don't. I suppressed my anger.

"If we wait to adopt, by the time we bring a baby in the house, I'll be too old. I won't have enough energy to take care of a baby. We need to do it now."

These discussions left us in a stalemate. We didn't have answers or a solution, and so we didn't move anywhere. The list of questions grew to the point of being completely overwhelming for both of us.

In vitro fertilization. How will hormone shots affect me, now and years from now? How do I feel about having a test tube baby? How invasive are the procedures? Will having a baby still be a sacred act? How many rounds would it take to be successful? Would we have the funds for multiple rounds?

Sperm donation. Is it cheating to use someone's sperm besides my husband; and if I do, how will that change the spiritual composition of a baby? How would we explain to our child that we used some-one else's sperm, and would they try to find him? How would we decide what sperm to use? Would we just ask a male friend or use a sperm bank?

Adoption. Will we even be considered because Barton has a disability? Will we be deemed good parents? What will we tell them when they grow older? Closed or open adoption? Would we adopt a baby with a disability, with an illness? What if we adopt and something happens to the baby, they get sick? Is it wrong to pay for a baby? How would it feel to "shop" for our own baby? Would I truly be able to interview and recognize red flags from a birth mother if we go through adoption on our own? Can we adopt if we are in debt?

Each possibility could be a fruitful avenue, and each also had its own concern and controversy, with it a set of personal, ethical, spiritual and physical dilemmas to sort through.

I have listened to many public debates over conception and adoption, but when it came to personal, internal beliefs as we considered each option, I was unprepared for the internal conflict, and how I felt I could not speak to anyone about these emotions.

Phases emerged. For about six months, I wanted to adopt right away. We visited an independent adoption agency just up the street from our house, met with an advisor and planned the next year to proceed. However, Barton became concerned about the economic challenges our family was facing, and I was terrified at the prospect of a home study.

We know regulations are in place to protect children of all nationalities, and that is our core belief; all children should be protected. I just couldn't help but think it was so unfair. Those who get pregnant naturally don't have someone inspecting their home or asking extremely personal questions, having to defend their points of view or their life history.

Timidly, I would call an adoption agency.

"Hi, I am interested in adopting a child. Do you work with families where a parent has a disability?"

I was met with a variety of responses.

One was, "Do you have life insurance?"

Another, "Well, if the other parent is healthy yes. We may have stipulations, like the disabled parent could never be alone with the child, or something like that."

I was dismayed when I heard, "What nationality are you looking at? We have different fees depending on the nationality."

I hung up the phone, confused and conflicted. Thoughts ran through my head. What would they think of us, a couple with a disability, who trained in martial arts? Would they go through my things? What if they deemed Barton could not be a good parent, even though when he is around children, his whole body lights up with excitement? How could we possibly justify every aspect about ourselves, seeking approval from someone else who had the power to tell us if we would be good parents or not.

When we looked at adoption, we were faced with all of these stipulations, legal requirements, places of acceptance and denial based purely on subjectivity. Did we have wills? Did we have life insurance? What about finances?

In the process of home studies, we were told every part of our lives would be looked at, how would having a baby impact our lives, and we would be questioned about our ability to bring a baby into a healthy environment. We kept delaying, afraid we didn't have everything in order and would be denied.

In addition, the laws for adoption are different in each state and in each country. We did an incredible amount of research on all of the different avenues from closed to semi-open to open adoption. Foster care would be a more economical option, but there is always the possibility that a child would be returned to their birth families.

We not only considered the expenses of adoption itself, but also the need for additional services: additional assistance for Barton, additional assistance for myself, and accessible equipment.

Knowing that we would need to rely on more community based services and local businesses, we began to brainstorm about how to get them involved in our family process. This would require a great deal of energy and time to create the close connections.

In another phase, we did consult with physicians who had been instrumental in making strides in IVF. Still, I was concerned about how the sacred process of having a baby could remain intact with the sterility of the medical office. To me, it was against everything I believed spiritually about how a soul comes into a woman's body.

I did consider all options. I spoke with another friend who talked about how harsh the medicine to induce ovulation was on the woman's body. She still was able to have children without any complications. Does it matter how it happens, or the end result only?

After the phase of adoption and IVF lost its appeal, we became intrigued with sperm donation because we knew only that Barton's imbalanced hormones were affecting fertility. I could conceive a child, even if it was through sperm donation. One weekend we discussed what would be important to us.

"Did you look through the available options?" I asked, "I would want to pick someone who has similar eyes. What did you think?"

"I would want someone who has a similar background to us."

"This one, his mother had Parkinson's. How much do we look at their family history?"

Then there was the question of siblings, and did the donor want to be contacted if the child wanted to know who their biological father was. Neither one of us knew how to make these decisions.

How much did social background, interests, or hobbies play a role? We would spend time discussing what characteristics and attributes were important to each of us and why, finally coming to a consensus of three that we would proceed with, once we were ready.

I had heard that the process in an infertility clinic was sterile, where the process was mere medical procedure. I couldn't fathom having the conception of a baby in such a detached and impersonal place.

Since we had no one to ask questions of about the best option or what we could expect, we were left to our own notions and judgments. We got just close enough to pursue this option, became frightened and retreated.

Instead, we found a birth and wellness center that offered individual rooms with soft light and an inviting environment for Barton and me, where we could have time afterwards, taking time to connect and relish the possibility of conception.

Though the success rate was small, only 5-10 percent, Barton and I began considering this method as a real possibility. The cost would be lower than adoption, and it would be more natural and less invasive than the IVF procedures.

Soon after, though, I became concerned. I was approaching 35, when a woman's body begins to change. While I know many women who have had children later in life, would I need to take hormones to have the best possible chance of success? Was the sperm sterilized? How is a spiritual being formed and created in the womb, and what contribution does each partner make?

Then there were reports of children who were looking for and found their biological fathers, who had many siblings. How awkward would it be to have my child meet siblings across the country? I became less enthusiastic about the idea of sperm donation.

There are some dreams we try so hard to remember and hold onto, but they always seem just beyond our grasp.

In addition, my need to have a child was in many ways wrapped up in my mother's passing. I remember when I was living with my mother just a year after graduating from college, standing in the kitchen making chocolate chip pancakes. My mother was sitting down, looking out of the window.

She smiled and turned toward me, "I can see you with two children someday. You are holding one around your waist, and the other is by your feet."

As I flipped pancakes, I could envision them too, wrapping my arms around a two-year old little girl with pigtails squirming in my arms, with the smell of coffee and pancakes lingering.

This dream dissipates like moisture in the air, yet returns briefly when I see my friends holding their children. My arms are still empty. If I became pregnant, I would feel what my mother had felt, bringing me closer to the maternal wonders of pregnancy.

It wasn't until we looked at some of these other options to conception that I was able to process my desires to have a baby, and my fears, my doubt and my anger that we couldn't have children. Once I saw the connection, I was able to let my mother go, along with the need to associate with my mother through pregnancy.

We also went through a difficult period with our friends and others who were concerned about our having children.

At a holiday party, I chatted on and on about our plans for adoption. "We have to figure out the finances, but we're really excited about open adoption."

I was asked, "What are your plans, how will you manage?"

I fumbled through, "Well, we've talked about the extra support Barton and I will need, and we're working on it."

"You know, you can't take care of a child all on your own. It's going to be hard work for you. I don't want to see you get so overwhelmed."

"I know, and we're looking at the help we would need."

"I know you both want children, but there is a reason God didn't give you a child. If God wanted you to have children, you would be pregnant by now. Why would you want to take care of someone else's child anyway?"

I stammered, at a loss for words, "I don't see it that way."

There were no words that came out of my mouth after that. What could I possibly say?

I left the room, searching for a corner to hide in. If I could just disappear, I wouldn't have to answer these questions. Why did I bring it up in the first place? I thought these were my friends, who would support me. I knew we had missing pieces, many missing pieces. But I thought our friends and family would help me figure out how to navigate through them, not tell us we shouldn't have children.

With those we knew, I would be questioned and have to justify how we could possibly take care of a child, similar to the ways in which I had to justify marrying someone with a disability. I would remember each comment, taking them personally.

I shrank inside myself. I could no longer hold my personal defenses, and I began to believe them. I lost myself, my confidence, my belief, and my faith. Even worse, Barton believed them, too.

In one discussion, held at our kitchen table, Barton said, "It's just not the right time. We need to get our finances worked out. I need to find a new job."

"We've always seen our family with children, and if we wait, I will be too old. There won't be enough time."

"I never wanted children." Barton responded.

In my mind I kept thinking, "But what about all those times we dreamed of them, talked about them."

Instead, I lashed out, "Maybe I should have never married you. I always wanted to be a mother. You knew that. Why did you let me marry you if you didn't want children?"

"Go on then, leave. I'm not holding you here. You don't need me. Go on and find someone else who can give you what you want."

Barton stormed out of the house, leaving me in the kitchen, face hot and red with tears.

To me, this was the worst kind of betrayal. After all, we had spent days dreaming and seeing children as a part of our lives together, and now he was telling me they were never part of our dream as a family.

When Barton returned, we didn't speak to each other. We could barely look at each other.

When Megan and I were dating, I remember spending hour upon hour on the phone telling her about dreams that I had of our children. We both saw our dreams as messages to guide us about our future life together.

For me, dreaming about our children, evening after evening, told me, at least so I thought, that we were to have our own biological children. We both embraced these dreams interpreting them literally. In many ways, these dreams also became a central component of beginning our lives together. It was only after I found out, if we had children, they would not come to us naturally, that I began to question my interpretation of my dreams.

Of course, this built upon the doubt that was already lingering in my mind from so many other aspects of life, from where I would find work, to finding my place in the community, to my role as a man.

With the mounting doubt, it became easier for me to deny what I had been shown than to open up to the possibilities that my limited human mind did not understand the full picture. This was an easy solution, and I embraced it wholeheartedly, turning my back on my wife and the dreams we had together. I know this tore deeply at her soul. I was unable to open up and communicate, and at that point, I was protecting my own wounds.

Before I could begin to open up and face not only those dreams that I had been denying but also the hurt I caused myself and the woman who I loved most deeply, I had to be willing to accept the value of my own life, regardless of whether or not this included producing sperm.

Because much of how I defined manhood was based on fertility, this discovery left me feeling incomplete and broken. How was I supposed to provide and protect our family, if I couldn't even create one? I turned toward my spirituality to provide a reason. Here, however, I only found more cause to blame myself. What had I done wrong to have this part of me taken away? Was their something in my family line that needed to end? If we found another way to have children, would we be going against God's will?

I have always believed there was a reason for my Cerebral Palsy, that it somehow served a purpose. Being a father was always a part of that purpose. Now, for the first time in many years, I felt incomplete. I did not understand what the purpose of my life was if I could not be a father.

Moreover, I failed Megan. I had promised her children. We both knew, or believed we knew, the path our lives were supposed to take. Without this major piece of the puzzle, what was left?

Many years ago, when I was 13 years old and going through puberty, I recall having a quiet sense that I could not produce sperm. Everything else functioned normally, and there was nothing tangible to support this feeling. But this nagging fear did not subside, and over time, I would occasionally ask my parents about this.

"Dad, sometimes I wonder if I have any sperm," I would say shyly, highly embarrassed to be approaching the subject with my father.

"What would make you say that, kiddo?"

"I don't know. I just wonder if everything's working right down there."

My dad answered plainly trying to be understanding, "Well, I don't see any reason for it not to be. The CP shouldn't affect that."

"I know it shouldn't, but it just… I don't know."

"I'm sure you have plenty of years to figure it out. Don't go trying to find out right now."

"I won't, Dad."

"I really don't think you have anything to worry about."

This conversation now haunted me; how could I have known so many years ago? What was I supposed to do with this memory? I believed somehow that all of my practice in meditation had rectified the issue and resolved whatever caused that feeling. It was clear this belief was wrong as well, and I was too ashamed to tell Megan.

I felt now that she had married me under false pretenses, and there was nothing I could do. I knew there was no way to give her what she wanted, and I began to believe she would be better off with someone else, someone who was a real man.

I had lost my way, and it wasn't until I was able to work through the numbness I was feeling that I could begin talking to Megan once again. At first, I was terrified. Our previous discussions around infertility and children left us both hurt and distrustful. Now, however, we would both have to show compassion to each other. Despite my willingness, I was still hesitant. Slowly, though, and in tiny snippets, we began to share with one another the burdens we had each been bearing.

"Megan, last night I had a dream about a baby again, for the first time in years."

"That's nice."

"I think we should talk about trying to figure out another way to have them."

Megan began picking up piles on the kitchen table to avoid eye contact. "I thought you didn't want kids anymore."

Taking a deep breath, I said, "I know I said that, and I'm really sorry. It was really hard to learn that I was the main reason we weren't getting pregnant. I didn't know who I was when that happened. I'm finding my way back, now. I remember who I am. I love you. I want to be with you, and I want children. I don't know if it's going to happen, but we won't know until we try. And I really want to try."

"Are you sure? How do I know that in another month, you're going to change your mind again?"

"You don't, and I know that. You have every right not to trust me after the way I hurt you. I'm asking for your trust now, anyway. Let me show you."

Megan sat down in a kitchen chair and looked at me, "Okay. So what's that mean?"

"I'm not sure. Can we figure it out together? I will tell you that over the past few months, adoption has resonated with me more and more. If I can't produce sperm, there is a reason, and I think it is so that we can take care of a child who needs a loving home. It feels like we can offer our home as a place for a child who comes into this world through another path and is in need of a loving and nurturing environment."

Megan moved to my lap and put her head on my shoulder, "Okay. I really want to experience pregnancy. It's just as much a part of my womanhood as producing sperm has been wrapped up in your manhood."

"I understand that, and I'm open to pursuing multiple avenues to give you that experience as well. But what I know at this moment is, after trying to understand why things happened this way, I feel like adoption is part of who we are. So many children don't have families, and our service together has always been to offer love where it is needed most. What better expression of that love is there than adoption?"

As we spoke more, I became aware that the space from which the desire to adopt arose was different than it had been previously. There seemed, at many levels, to be a lessened attachment to the outcome. While the desire to have children remained, it was no longer a vital component of my innate wholeness as a human being and as a man.

Alone, in the middle of the night, I journaled about femininity, motherhood, and maternity.

> Pregnancy is about life giving, providing the space to nurture a soul, it is what we were meant to do. The ability to have children. Every time I get my cycles, I think—what a waste. Wasteful. I am being wasteful. It's not about my connection with my mother—it's about connection with motherhood—the column to God, the vessel, life giving, Changing Woman. Being separate, barren is cutting off from that flow. Wasting that flow. This loss is the loss of connection, of flow, of trust. No matter what we do, we can never go back to those dreams of having a family.

I was vulnerable, but I shared some of my writing with Barton, which led to the most incredible conversations about sharing our loss with each other. During this time, we began to grieve together. In this raw sadness, slowly, we began to hold hands, talk, and find connection with each other.

There are still times when I believe those who have told us we should never have children, when I don't believe we will bring a child into our home. Barton has been the one to carry the dream when I have given up. He has found the joy of smiling and playing with children who are not our own.

One day at the grocery store, a 3- or 4-year-old was sitting in a shopping cart as his mother was perusing the aisle. As we passed, the boy asked Barton, "What's wrong with you? Why are you in a chair?"

Barton beamed, "Hi, I'm Barton. I have Cerebral Palsy. You know when you talk on the phone, there's a connection between two people. Well, for me, it's like that connection has static, and my muscles can't always 'hear' what my brain is saying. So I use a chair to get around."

For twenty minutes, Barton chatted with this boy who was so curious and asked many questions.

Whether it's smiling at a child in a restaurant or a friend's child who crawls up the wheelchair into his lap, Barton uses these opportunities to enjoy being around children. He still holds the possibility that we will have children, someday.

For many years after we moved into our home in Raleigh, the extra room in the back of the house was kept empty, just in case.

It wasn't until last year that we transformed it into my office. Though we are now using the totality of our home as we should, there is still a part of me that dreams of rocking a child to sleep in my mother's rocking chair, surrounded by baby yellow walls in the middle of the night.

I feel you near me
moving to the flow of light,
we are flying,
soaring the skies.
For a time,
we are blending,
for I move within you
and you with me.
Stirring the soul,
we hold each other
up to the moon,
soaring the stars,
seeing the earth,
the eye of our souls.
raindrops fall
to the earth below
and we return
to the sun,
encasing our intertwined
souls filled with light.

~ Megan M. Cutter, 2003

Chapter Thirteen

Dents, Dings and Damage

I often wonder who taught Megan how to drive a chair, and then my curiosity quickly turns to an amused embarrassment as I remember. It was me, and while I do have some moments of lucidity in my driving, I, for the most part, am a maniac on wheels. Whether I like to admit it or not, somewhere in my wallet rests a faded copy of my crackerjack license.

I've never been one for vanity, particularly when it comes to the interior of a house. I suppose, given my wheelchair driving record, this is a good thing. Since I've been in a power chair, you would think that in the nearly thirty years of driving, I would have learned to avoid a wall. Nevertheless, I continue to be struck by walls that jump out at me from nowhere.

This was particularly challenging growing up in Nancy's house, where she valued interior design and perfection. I noticed after a year of living together she insisted on having the walls repainted every six months. Somehow, my driving became the enemy of her esthetic expression. She soon found a way around this, however, after beginning to work as an architect for a nursing home facility—she installed rubber bumpers along the floorboards of my dad's house. When I left for school, I knew the walls in my dorm and in my apartment complex would never survive my path of destruction.

The first time Megan visited me in Tucson, I recall giving her a driving lesson in the middle of the spacious University of Arizona Quad. She got into my lap and took control of the joystick, her initial maneuver propelled us head on into the only biker within a half-mile radius. This, my dear friends, was Megan's first attempt at driving a power wheelchair.

During that visit, I learned the truth about how she drives. As we toured the campus, there were moments where she mistrusted herself at the wheel, bumping into an occasional curb and laughing at me as if I were nuts for allowing her to drive.

After that first brush with fate, however, it did not take her long to find the delicate touch needed to steer, at least in wide-open spaces. It wasn't long before we were racing through an empty parking deck on the edge of campus to catch the sunset over the Tucson mountains.

When I invited her to try to drive my chair into the bedroom, she looked at me quizzically asking, "Are you sure?"

I said, "Yes. Go ahead."

She took my control and skimmed by just barely nicking the edge of the door as it lay open against the adjacent wall. I was impressed, I must admit. There was only an additional scuffmark at the time, and I thought perhaps she was far more talented at driving my chair than even I was after my whole life.

After a day of playing out in the desert sun, we returned home and I got out of my wheelchair. I asked Megan if she could put it in the bedroom so it would be out of our way. As she climbed in and grabbed hold of the joystick, Megan inadvertently knocked it into a higher gear, one which I often use to train in martial arts.

She plowed toward the doorway, missing the entrance and catching the edge of the door itself, tearing the laminate panel off the front of the door, ripping it like a sheet of paper from the frame.

She burst out in hysterics, "Oh my God, Barton. I'm so sorry!"

I was sitting on the sofa, which faced my bedroom door watching this fiasco unfold before me. The mortified look on her face told me that she obviously thought this was some horrible incident, one that could never be rectified.

I erupted in laughter losing my balance and falling sideways onto the couch and then down to the floor in hysterics. Megan's demeanor also opened up realizing this was just par for the course and would have its place within our relationship.

It wasn't long before we had grown used to the dents and dings during the time I lived with her in her mother's house. Though, during our time there, I only recall one incident where my wheelchair took a toll on the house.

Megan was so mortified because I had accidently rammed my chair into the bedroom wall creating a two by three inch hole, much too large for a simple spackling job. She called her father, who graciously agreed to drive over from Atlanta to teach me how to repair dry wall. These skills were to come in handy later in life.

Years later, after we had settled into our new house in the piedmont of central North Carolina, we again ran into doorways that were a mere thirty inches wide.

We were delighted to have bought a home in Raleigh that met nearly all of our needs in a way that was certainly beyond our imaginings. Even so, the holes are inevitable as our hallway is nearly as narrow as the doors themselves, making it difficult to pass, even in my most concentrated periods of driving.

Today, we have a running bet on who makes the largest hole and how many holes each of us can make. I'm sure this bet will grow substantially, but at the moment I believe both Megan and I are at a fairly even standing with many holes apiece.

Now, you have to understand, when I say hole, I am referring to any instance where the force of the impact has broken through both sides of the drywall and has left a miniature window into the inner workings of our house. Certainly nothing less than this is even worth bothering to mention.

Perhaps the most amusing incident concerning my wheelchair and our less than perfect driving record happened, in fact, while I was in the bathroom. Megan tried to bring my wheelchair into the bedroom from the hall. I sat patiently and waited as I listened to her drive down the hallway. Once she reached the bedroom door, I began hearing all sorts of bangs and dings against the doorframe.

A minute later, there was a loud crash, and I distinctly heard the words, "Oh shit!"

I didn't even have time to wonder what happened; Megan hurtled across the bedroom floor in my wheelchair and slammed into the wall opposite our door.

"What on earth happened?" I exclaimed.

All Megan could do was laugh, and I sat bewildered pants down on the toilet trying to surmise how on earth she managed to ram the wheelchair into the wall. After she got me up off the toilet and into my chair, we both perused the situation.

Clearly, Megan was having trouble getting through our door. Somehow she tore the door itself off its hinges and was laughing so hard, she forgot to remove her hand from the control. How this happened, I had no idea. Into the opposite wall she careened. In her wake, there was a three-inch by four-inch hole at the base of the wall right above the molding: absolutely beautiful as far as holes go.

Later on, Megan claimed this entire mishap was due to the differing dimensions between my new wheelchair and the old one she had grown accustomed to driving. According to her, not only was this wheelchair longer and more bulky, but the Combat Mode provided more *umph* to its maneuverability. Even so, how this translates directly into tearing a door completely from its hinges, I will never know.

Over the years, it has brought me great joy to watch Megan shift her perspective of what it means to have a beautiful and loving home. Much like my stepmother, she grew up to believe that the physical appearance of a home's interior was the trademark sign of elegance and beauty.

In the years we have lived together, however, her need to cling to perfect physical appearance has loosened. In its place, she has redefined the true value of a home, by its feeling of warmth, especially when it is peppered by moments of outrageous laughter.

In particular, her ability to laugh at our ongoing bet says much about her own growth. Our mutual reliance on humor has expanded beyond the realm of our house and serves as a grounding point for the both of us to accept one another's foibles as well as our own.

Often, we find that we are able to rely on the other one to laugh at us, not in a degrading sense, but in a way that reveals to us what we are unable to see for ourselves. In doing so, this lightness of heart enables us to let go more fully.

Sure, there is much pleasure in having a space we could call our own, which is filled with the laughter and love that we have always brought into it, but it seemed to me there needed to be a deeper more substantial reason.

While our first reason to own our own home in the first place was to have children, I soon realized that this was only part of the picture. The current reality for many people with disabilities is that home ownership exists far beyond their reach.

No, home ownership for people with disabilities is certainly not unheard of, but it is not what one might consider to be the norm. Instead, most "best case scenarios" are having someone live independently in an apartment or with a roommate. However, most people are still living in group homes.

How then, I wondered, does having a home of our own offer those we work with the opportunity to dream of what may be possible for them as well? The holes in the wall and scuff marks across the oven facing have come to be reminders for me that the chance to have our own home is a unique blessing few are in a position to experience.

At the same time, with each client, be it a person with a disability or an entire family, we are offering them a broader perspective of what may be possible for their own lives. The simple gifts that come from the opportunity to be an example for others lightens my heart and makes me smile with every hole that we patch.

As for our house, as long as it continues to serve its purpose, despite being adorned with a nick here or a hole there, I hope those who visit discover some of the humor and joy that we've shared with one another.

Communion
Six o'clock and dawn is not yet sprung as a
battery of raindrops pounds a melody
against the window pane.

The bitter smell of damp hay
rouses me like sounds from a November fireplace.
I stir semi-lucid between flannel sheets like a newborn
blindly searching for his mother's absent nipple.

Your form, descending from heaven to rest at my side,
illuminates the dawn as we draw close.

~ S. Barton Cutter, October 2003

Chapter Fourteen

What, No Money from the Money Tree?

Once settled in North Carolina, Barton worked for a grant-funded project, and I took my time stepping back into the workplace. I didn't want to return to the corporate world, but I couldn't just journal in my notebook all day either. I found smaller contracts here and there, administrative work, writing press releases or folding and mailing newsletters. I could feel there should be more purpose to my work, but I just didn't know what it was yet.

And there was another looming monster beginning to bear down on our shoulders. The move from Alabama was incredibly expensive, and while we sold many of the furnishings that collected dust in my mother's house, we were still creating a deficit. We sold the house I inherited from my mother, but the same square footage cost double in Raleigh. We weren't prepared for the difference.

After we moved, I couldn't help but take out the credit card and swipe it for the many necessities we needed to begin our lives in North Carolina. We also enjoyed traveling, training several days of the week which required an hour drive each way, and training away from home. At first, I didn't think about the cost of gas as we drove from place to place.

Before long, however, I knew what we were doing. I could see the hotel room charges, the restaurant bills, accessible van rental fees, and training fees all stacking up. Barton was so excited about being in a place where we could train twice a week, and be so involved in traveling and going to seminars. I just didn't have the heart to tell Barton no, and Barton didn't ask.

Since Barton was not on federal or state disability benefits, we also had many discussions about how to pay for help in the mornings to get Barton out of bed, dressed and ready to go for the day. At first, we used college students, but they were not always reliable. We struggled to maintain the out-of-pocket expenses, which were almost as expensive as our mortgage.

I remember my mother, who lived with Multiple Sclerosis and struggled to maintain an independent life, still relying on state disability services to get through the month. Even though her energy level varied from day to day, on days when she was feeling better, she would have to stay in bed or at home in fear that a care provider would come by, report she did not need services and she would lose the support she did need.

When we were married, Barton no longer qualified for these federal or state disability services, and we had to figure out how we would fill in the gaps, the places where Barton does need additional assistance. In the end, we couldn't justify this cost, and I took on the routine of getting Barton up in the mornings.

I would wake up in the middle of the night with thoughts of our survival racing through my mind. I had to get out of bed to mull over the numbers in the checking account, even if it was 3 in the morning. I stared at the computer screen, at what we had in our accounts, or what we didn't have, assessed the stack of bills not yet mailed, and tried to figure out how to make it all balance out.

Even after we moved into our house, we didn't talk about how we were going to pay for all of the expenses we were incurring. We were processing so many other aspects of our marriage, hoping to start a family, looking at new prospects for work, and writing. Finances just seemed to be too hard to add into the discussions.

One Tuesday evening in February of 2007, we were in the car driving to martial arts training in Durham. I could tell something was on Barton's mind by the furl on his brow, and I picked up on the tension that seemed to be between us. I couldn't take it anymore.

"What's going on?"

"My contract ends in two weeks. They said my contract would be renewed; they said they would find a permanent position for me, but they didn't. My contract goes away at the end of February."

The entire car must have reverberated with my scream and the long string of expletives that followed.

Barton tried to get a sentence in. "We'll figure something out."

"What? How are we going to pay the mortgage? How are we going to eat? You've got to be kidding me."

"We've done it before. I know it'll be hard, but we'll be okay."

"I just can't do this anymore. I'm done. I'm so done with this."

Barton couldn't get the words out. "What do you want me to do to fix it?"

"I don't know. How am I supposed to know? You're supposed to have a job."

Our voices fell silent. We had no answers.

While Barton dug his heels in to find a writing contract to do virtually anything, I tried to balance the books. It wasn't any use; there just wasn't enough coming it. We put more and more living expenses on credit including gas, groceries, and we even used credit to pay for credit, and we fell into a dark and deep financial hole.

I found a job as a receptionist, which only lasted a few months, and Barton found little writing contracts here and there. We would choose which bills we could pay, and which would have to be late.

"Barton, you have to find another contract. We're just not going to make it," I said. This only contributed to the mounting anxiety between us.

My habit of getting up early to look at the daily bank accounts grew into a compulsion, and just thinking about what we needed would make my stomach ache.

Finally, Barton was able to secure a new writing contract, and while it was renewable after a year, fear would still take hold of me in the middle of the night. In the glow from my computer screen, I would stare at the bank account numbers.

We were three years into our marriage and balancing tiny contracts just to survive. It was also the year of Barton's surgery and a much needed roof-replacement. The money hole grew deep and slippery. We are still climbing out of it. We hit the limit of every credit card we had, and still we found ourselves with car repairs, doctor bills, unexpected expenses, and ones which we had no way to pay back.

One month, I forgot to pay a credit card, and received calls from the creditor three times a day. I would see their number on my phone and slam the phone down. Each time they called, I was visibly shaking from fear, of what I would say, of how we would pay for the bill.

"Barton, I've had enough. We're pulling it all out on the table. We have to make a change. I'm not doing this again."

That weekend, we called a financial advisor, and began looking at our options. While we didn't qualify to refinance our mortgage, we did reorganize our payment priorities and began the process of paying off one bill at a time. I sold our dining room table, a credenza, extra chairs, and some other odds and ends to an auctioneer. We moved to a cash system, pulling cash out at the beginning of the month and made envelopes for different categories: groceries, gas, dining out, personal funds.

We also began to look at where we were spending our funds, and like most people, dining out became a huge expense. So, for a while, I would balk any time Barton picked something up, until I realized it was Barton's way of taking care of me. If I had a rough day or was exhausted, he may not be able to cook a meal, but he could go out and pick something up for us. We began to take that into consideration, allowing for those expenses.

While we still went out on Friday nights, our date night together at a local pizza restaurant, we also cooked in the kitchen. One Sunday afternoon, we pulled out spices for a delicious vegetable lasagna.

"More mozzarella," Barton said. We loved making a Parmesan cheese crusted top, and I would add pieces of kale.

"You got the last bite of the top layer. It's my turn," we quibbled over the last bite.

Our first month on a cash-only system we both felt relieved; we were taking responsibility for where we were and how to get out of the hole we were in. It wasn't until this place, where I felt like we could breathe again, that I realized how much responsibility I took on for the finances.

One Saturday morning, we sat down together to write bills as a couple. I went on about my own ordinary routine of writing numbers out in a row, adding them up, and calculating by mumbling to myself.

Barton sat beside me in the kitchen. "Love, what are you doing?"

"I'm doing the bills," I put down my pen and looked at him.

"Yes, I know. I thought you wanted my help."

"You are helping."

"No, I'm just sitting here beside you. You're doing the bills."

"Okay, can you look it over after I finish writing?" I had a system after all, a pile for bills to be paid now, and a pile to wait a few weeks. I had my color post-it notes out to write down the amount, check number, and due date to go on the outside of the envelope.

"Sure, that's perfect."

I picked up the pen and kept writing my list of expenses, "Here you go." I handed my notebook to Barton, who looked over my scribbled notes.

"I think we're going to need to transfer $2,000," I continued, "but I'm not sure I added that right. And here's the column of cash we need to pull out. We also need the car repaired this month, too. It looks like we might have to wait a few weeks."

Barton looked up, "Do you want my help, or not?"

Barton was willing, and wanting to take this on, but in some ways, I wasn't letting him. I kept trying to do it all myself.

Opening the dialogue of finances affected us in more ways than just talking about money. It brought us closer and enabled us to explore other areas that we had previously been unwilling to share.

When Barton was looking at working with a disability provider to offer mentorship and coaching, we visited several group homes and day programs, as I was hoping to offer creative expression workshops as well.

As we entered the facility, I noticed how everyone moved in a group together, and the support staff instructed each person in what they should be doing, nearly every moment we were there. I listened to the staff members talk about the care that each person received.

We also visited the art classes and learned that many times, paintings and artwork was sold to keep programs going. Yet, the artists themselves received little compensation for their work.

A staff member told me, "Each person receives one hour a month on their own with a support staff member to explore their own interests."

One hour. I could sit at a coffee shop for one hour, and it would feel like just a few minutes. One hour on their own, and at every other moment, they are in a group with people they may or may not like, with little choice about what activity they would do. This image of one hour shocked and profoundly impacted me.

I would think, "One hour. What if I only had one hour. What would I do?"

How much do we take our own freedom for granted; many of us do not even think about freedom and choice during the course of our lives.

Barton and I have seen youth and adults working hard to make the leap into full independence, but for one reason or another cannot sustain it. They may fall back, relying on disability providers, federal and state programs, or other community day programs.

While the cultural paradigm has shifted to a value based perspective, moving youth and adults with disabilities out of institutions, the focus is still on basic needs, food, living arrangements, and transportation.

As much as we wanted to mentor and educate individuals and professionals about how to make positive choices, and thinking independently through experiential learning, many communities just aren't ready to address these issues.

Processing these experiences, I began to value Barton in a new way. In looking at the very beginning of our relationship, I realized how Barton researched and navigated us through everything from health insurance to moving across state lines and what we should do after he lost disability benefits. His role was essential in taking care of all of these pieces, and it wasn't until much later when I understood how much responsibility Barton took on, without my even realizing it.

In many respects, it may have been easier to have had a commitment ceremony instead of a marriage ceremony. But what we have gained by allowing ourselves to follow our hearts and step beyond other's expectations of Barton's need to rely on federal benefits, has enabled us to find work positions that we live, build our own sustainability, experience both the highs and the lows of living without a safety net, and has forced us to face harsh realities and persevere through them.

We also ensure that after one of us passes away, the other will be taken care of through traditional provisions, rather than being turned over to the state.

As hard as we have struggled through our own financial difficulties, we are considered a success. I would have never been exposed to this feeling of valuing our own independence if we had not visited these other paradigms of living.

Barton pointed out to me on numerous occasions how remaining optimistic, even while we faced financial challenges allowed us to flow through them with more ease.

Eventually, I let go of looking into our bank accounts every morning, and trusted we have what we need. We scheduled weekly meetings to review the budget, wrote checks together and worked through unexpected financial hits such as house or car repairs.

We still have dreams of what we can't afford right now, an accessible van, growing our family, and we trust in each other that someday, we will find a way through the challenges to reach them.

At night, we now lie in bed together holding hands, "I am thankful for you, how much you make me laugh. For getting through the day. For having work to do, for the feeling of abundance. I am thankful to be alive, for being here with you."

"I am thankful for God, for being with you. For this day, and what will come tomorrow."

With pulsing breath,
into the subtle we venture-
two phoenix yearning;
our faith leavens as hands clasp into one.

We are not known by form,
only a faint gasp,
distant rhythm of a palpated drum,
inspires our skyward waltz.

~ S. Barton Cutter. 2004

Chapter Fifteen

Losing the Way

A year and a half after my surgery, I found myself in the kitchen rummaging through a drawer desperate to find a blade. I had never held a knife before, always afraid I would cut myself unintentionally. But now, that was precisely my intent.

When I found one, the control of my hand as it wrapped around the handle surprised me. I was frightened to the point where the motor control of my hand and the sensitivity of its nerves, were heightened. I drew the knife from the drawer, ironically, being careful not to hurt myself before the intended moment.

Once drawn, I clasped the hilt with the other hand for added support, and inspected the blade sharpness with careful intent. Satisfied that it would do the job, I pointed it clearly at my throat, and noticed the light reflecting on the tip.

My breath calmed as I slowly brought the blade toward my neck, believing this would be my final moment on this earth. I imagined how brief the pain would be as I inserted the blade. As I drew the knife closer, the thought intensified.

I paused for a moment. Reconnecting with the conviction that if only

I could be swift in my execution, all would be fine. I raised the knife again to the edge of my skin, but the thought of impending pain once again stopped me in my tracks. I knew now that such an act was not one that I could bring myself to carry out.

I threw the knife down. My hands trembled. There was nothing left in me, but the incomprehensible urge to survive. I went outside to catch some air.

My heart pounding through my chest, I wondered how I got here, and more importantly what it was that stopped me from taking my life. I wish I could say in that moment that there was some divine revelation; the hand of God reaching down and showing me the vastness of His glory. No, it was nothing so spectacular, only the innate human impulse to continue living.

I wondered about this, questioning myself as to what purpose this served. Yes, the impulse was to survive, and at the same time, I could find no reason but to continue serving other people. I sat on the porch for an hour trying to calm my nerves and understand the ramifications of this choice to live. The past year and a half had been devastating.

I didn't know how I had gotten here. All I knew was that Megan and I seemed to always be fighting over training, over finances, over what our family was to look like.

Little by little, the purpose for my life that I had once believed in so adamantly had melted away, leaving a blackened void in the center of my soul.

It began nearly a year before the surgery, when a job that I believed to be a divine calling lost its funding. I was released, searching for another position and taking my only refuge within martial arts classes.

At the same time, I was unaware of many issues within our family. I had turned my back on our finances, and Megan sought to protect us by not sharing the financial picture that we found ourselves in. While all of this was going on, there was also great change occurring among friends from the martial arts group that I had grown to consider my family.

Now this group of friends was splitting apart, and Megan had lost her desire to participate in the community after a falling out with some of our closest friends. She then doubted everything she was capable of, which was only compounded by my refusal to acknowledge what she was experiencing.

One of the most common disagreements revolved around getting to or from training itself. Class was forty-five minutes away from our home, and in order to get there at seven, we would often leave around six. Pick up dinner on the way, eat quickly, putting our expenses on non-existent credit, train for two and half hours and then leave at 10 pm to return home.

Excited about training, I chatted, "Wasn't that a great class tonight? You have to learn to pick up the intent and drop it immediately."

"You don't have to yell at me," Megan huffed. She gripped the steering wheel. "I hate driving so late, I can't see anything."

"I wasn't yelling," I said with a surprised recoil, my body tightened as my arm spasmed, bumping Megan's elbow.

"Yes you are, and don't hit me. I don't have to drive you, you know. I have to get up at four am tomorrow. Why can't you find a ride to training?" The car veered in and out of lanes as waves of emotion swept across Megan.

"Calm down. You almost had the technique. All you had to do was…"

"Can you talk to me? I need you to keep me awake."

"I am talking to you. What do you want me to say?" Falling silent, I gazed out the window, noticing headlights flash in and out of the side view mirror.

"It'd be nice to get home at a reasonable hour for once."

"Sorry. Damn, what's your problem?"

I knew what was coming. "I have to get up at four am every morning, and here we are, it's midnight. We're going to get home and get in bed at two," Megan rambled.

"Fine. Forget this. I just won't ask. Why did I open my mouth? I was just trying to talk."

Megan said trying to deescalate the conversation, "Well, tell me something that happened today."

"Screw this. I just want out of the car. Let me out of the car."

"Come on Barton, that's ridiculous."

"You know what's ridiculous? Yea, let me out right now. I don't want any part of this."

While two and a half hours of class time provided a moment of refuge, our car rides to and from training often ended in yelling matches. Any passing comment from Megan, I interpreted as a personal attack, and Megan seemed to always be tired and frustrated.

How is it that two people who have drastically different experiences of the same community find common ground if they are unwilling to discuss the whole of each other's perspective? This was the situation we found ourselves in.

I knew she was struggling to find her place, and I felt guilty for feeling so at home in this community. Training in martial arts itself provided me with the tools to navigate the transitions we were facing. At the same time, I was so unwilling to deal with my own complexity of emotion, the relief and insight gained in class was quickly undone by my own refusal to show Megan the compassion she needed.

I also bought into the belief our inability to have children naturally was somehow a divine message telling us not to pursue parenthood in any form. This view came with a natural ease, which for Megan, undermined everything we were as a couple.

In our earlier years, we had dreamed at great length about our own children and what it would be like to be parents. How, despite my disability, we would discover ways to bring them up as strong and happy youth. I had never believed there might be a possibility our visions would play out differently than how we perceived them through our conversations.

When the results from our doctors returned showing natural conception was not an option, it was easier for me to deny the dream of parenthood as much as it was easy for me to misplace my trust in my manhood.

An off the cuff comment would incite a firestorm from either side, usually when we were in the car or while I sat immobile in the bathroom. The tensions in the house were always heightened, guards always up, neither of us trusting the other to lend a compassionate ear.

A question as simple as, "What is the schedule for tomorrow?" made me feel trapped and insecure.

The only thing I knew to do was do fight back. Any anger I felt towards Megan, I turned on myself and completely shut down.

Over time, I grew wary of the heightened hostility, and in an attempt to diffuse the fight, I also began to abdicate my power. Indeed, some of this had already begun unconsciously. Unsure of where to go after losing my first real job and discovering I was the sole reason our dreams of children would not be realized. But you're not!

I sat numb for months at a time, unable to make a decision of any consequence, and when others tried to assist me, I would lash out in rage.

Sadly, this is not an uncommon scenario among people within the disability community. So often, a culture of disempowerment is perpetuated as much by those with disabilities as it is by those who come in contact with them.

As relationships form, the dynamics between independence and dependence clash. On the one hand, the desire to be completely independent conflicts with the security of dependency.

The risks of stepping outside of one's comfort zone seems too great, the feeling of being a burden leads to guilt, and one can feel trapped.

One afternoon before training, I asked, "Can I get a ride to class?" Megan looked up from her computer with an overwhelmed expression.

"Never mind," I quickly recanted, "I don't need to train."

"I can take you if you want."

"No, it's too much for you. Don't worry about it." My mind was made up.

"Barton, if you need to go to training, just say so. It's not a big deal today."

"Why, so we can fight on the way home? Yea, that's fun." I felt my chest tighten.

Megan closed her laptop, "It really is okay. If you need to train, then train."

"I don't want to make you drive all that way, it's too much for you. I'm too much for you. All I do is get in your way. Why did you marry me?" I clasped my hands together and doubled over in my chair holding my stomach unable to listen or speak.

Whatever Megan said in response, I didn't hear. In many ways, I wanted to stay stuck in the helpless position that I had created, and then blamed everyone around me for placing me in that position.

Over the months, this cycle worsened to the point where nothing in life brought me joy. Because of my unwillingness to accept responsibility for the position I found myself in, I numbed my soul from the emotions of anger and sorrow. I looked out into a world of gray and saw nothing worth preserving.

Now, resting on the porch after staring down the cold face of my own death, I found a glimmer of humanity buried in the rubble of shame and guilt. Uncovering it was like discovering a relic of the ancient past, precious in origin and serving a higher yet still unknown purpose.

I sat, feeling the cool breeze caress my skin, and noted the quiet damp grass that swayed on the lawn below. Life was tangible again: immediate and vibrant.

But what of me? What was the relevance of this one life? Yes, my survival instinct had awakened. Something deep within sparked like flint against a cold hardened rock. I was offered a glimpse into seeing this humanity once more.

Now it was up to me to understand the full range of my personal experience, and use these experiences to empower others with their own sense of capacity to contribute.

In the following weeks, this emergence out of darkness grew in me as a divine gift. I knew in order to understand the full implications of my life purpose, I had to nurture it to my full capacity and then offer this understanding of the value and importance of each person to others.

With this increasing sense of revelation, and after much work to rebuild a healthy foundation personally and in my relationship to Megan, we began exploring what our purpose was in the world together.

My love, your eyes golden chocolate
sparkle in opal reflections
that permeate my soul.
Tangerine confectioned teeth lap
sweetly, blowing opulent hew.
I taste the nectar of your breath and sing
honeysuckled java upon your lips
tasting bittersweet on my tongue.

We wrap ourselves leg in leg,
your pelvis tight against mine,
yearns to hum soft in its vibrant tone.

I breathe ecstasy
and collapse into you
like the hummingbird beckoning a new blossom.

~ S. Barton Cutter, February 14, 2011

Chapter Sixteen

Wheels in Revelation

While I took a break from training, realizing the late night drives were not healthy for me, I also began to look at our personal and professional work. As an artist, I was particularly frustrated because of the conflict between work and service, how to make a living and at the same time not give up my dream as a writer.

I had also fallen into a place where the world looked gray, and I could see no way to reach our goals of having a family, providing for our family and doing what I loved so much.

Through a woman's social networking group, I was introduced to the concept of professional life coaching, someone who would work with me one-on-one to tackle these challenges.

In these coaching sessions, I realized many emotional cycles created from my childhood were affecting my belief about myself, and the way I interacted with the different communities we were a part of including our martial arts group, our writing group and the local disability community.

I also realized how much Barton and I were bouncing off of each other, reacting to each other's emotions in ways of which we weren't even conscious.

For example, just before leaving for a writing event, I balked, "We're going to be late. We're not going to make it. What are we going to do?"

"Come on, let's go."

I frantically ran around the house, "I can't find the keys."

"Well, I don't know where they are. They have to be in the house somewhere."

I looked in the bedroom, office, bathroom. I fumbled through bills on the kitchen table. I sighed, exasperated. "I have so much to do today. There's no way I can get all of it done."

"You know what, forget it. We're not going. It's not worth it." I could tell Barton was upset by his arms spasming out to the side.

"But I want to go." I had been planning on this event for a long time.

"Fine, let's go, but you can't have it both ways."

"What?" I would ask, not understanding Barton. Typically, if we were in a discussion or a hurry, I would not understand Barton's speech pattern, too caught up in my own thoughts.

We both knew these patterns weren't healthy, but we didn't know how to change them. Through coaching, I began to identify my negative self-talk and how it impacted our relationship, which then blended into our work and outside relationships.

Knowing that we could both benefit from coaching, for a time, Barton and I would see a coach together.

We began to wade through the challenges surrounding work, children and personal direction with our coach. This process gave the space to explore the individual choice to embrace my life, appreciating both challenges and successes equally. This exploration allowed me to clarify my core values and enabled me to use them as a foundation upon which to build.

More importantly, it also provided a safe space for Megan and me to relearn how to communicate with one another. I noticed our personal transformation and how we were able to relate and connect to one another in ways that we had not done in years. Here, the seeds of compassion took root and we each began to remember why we fell in love with one another.

As we found our way back to stable footing in our relationship, it became increasingly apparent to me that I needed to look at what brought me joy in my life, beyond my relationship with Megan.

With this insight, I began returning to training and also began searching for ways to contribute to the world in a way that was meaningful to me. From our personal experience of working with a coach to rebuild our relationship, I saw the potential that other families could benefit through a similar process.

I began looking for a coaches' training program that would offer the appropriate credential and was also compatible with my experiences and practices. It did not take long before I found one that seemed to be a good fit.

I knew the program I had chosen was the right one, but registering for classes did not happen as easily as I expected.

I should know by now that every time I attempt something new, whether it is me alone or with Megan, we inevitably seem to break down inaccurate perspectives of people with disabilities.

However, I expected that the people who worked for the coaching program would be more receptive to my participating.

Excited by the chance to pursue this newly emerging dream, I sat down with Megan and called to register. We were on speakerphone so that Megan could assist in translating for me if necessary.

"Registration, how may I help you?"

"Hi, yes, I'd like to register for both the basic and intermediate coaching classes." I looked at Megan to interpret for me.

"Hi, this is Barton Cutter, and I'm his wife, Megan. Sometimes it's hard to understand Barton on the phone so I'm here to lend a hand. He would like to register for both the basic and intermediate coaching classes."

"Okay," the voice said on the other end of the line, "and that's all five courses?"

"Yes, that's correct," I interjected.

"Yes," Megan echoed.

"One second, please," the woman responded. After a few minutes, another lady picked up, "Hi, I'm told that you're interested in registering for some coaching classes."

I explained again with excitement in my voice.

There was a long pause. "Are you sure this is the right path for you? It may be difficult for others to understand you and coaching is about helping others along their path of self-discovery. That'll be hard if they don't understand you." She was choosing her words carefully. She was trying to remain respectful, but the quiver in her voice revealed to us her discomfort with being in uncharted territory.

"Yes, I know that, that's exactly what coaching is about. I'm here to be a coach. I have no doubt that I can do it." Megan repeated my words, just in case the woman didn't understand me.

"Okay, well, I would hate for you to register for all of them and find out after the first one that it's not going to work. Could I convince you to just sign up for the first one and see what happens? Then, if it still feels right, you could go on and do the others."

My heart sank, but I understood where she was coming from. So I agreed. When we hung up, Megan commented, "That's so interesting. I could pick up on her fear, it was coming through the phone lines."

At the first session, and in part due to my own need to regain stability and confidence, I asked Megan to accompany me in order to translate should the need arise.

The class was given an exercise to coach an instructor in somewhat of a free for all, and about half way through the exercise, I felt something turn on inside of me. I switched my wheelchair on and prepared myself.

When the opportunity arose, I tore from my space to the front of the room and engaged with the teacher so clearly and openly that I actually have no recollection of what I said. What I do remember, however, is the sensation of knowing something I had not experienced in years: a conviction that I could just move and act, trusting, without thought, that whatever came was exactly what was needed for the other person.

Later Megan told me, "When you got up to coach Griffin, I could see your face light up. I saw you come back into the man I saw when we first met. Everyone in the room was affected by your intensity." When she began talking, there were tears in her eyes, and I could tell she meant what she said.

I now had rediscovered a feeling of personal freedom and intensity that comes from expressing the fullness of who I am, and I knew precisely how to replicate it. From this experience, I recognized a foundation from which to forge a new and integrated practice for serving others.

For me, learning how to trust myself again has come in moments of clarity interspersed with periods of stumbling and learning to recover gracefully. There have still been moments of doubt, however, as I grow in my awareness, I have come to hold a greater faith in my own ability to grow. I see now that the doubt is not representative of who I am. I soon began utilizing tools from previous training, integrating them into my coaching practice.

As I continued to rediscover my individual passions for life, and a renewed purpose for living, Megan and I also began to go through a transformation within our relationship, one that opened the doors to new levels of communications and a profound support and love for one another permeated all that we did together.

While I witnessed Barton beginning to come back, my journey came in fits and spurts. I did not know where the paths would lead, but I was also determined not to give up.

For a while, I stepped back from the groups we were a part of, specifically training in our martial arts group. I was tired of complaining about getting home so late and having only three to four hours of sleep every night. I had also grown resentful of this group, how Barton was receiving support and training, but I wasn't, not in the ways I needed anyway.

Since I was getting Barton up in the mornings, working and taking care of house chores, I found myself exhausted. The reality was, I couldn't do it all, but there wasn't anyone to talk to about how to fill in the missing pieces.

One winter, I collapsed on the sofa every evening and every weekend. I had no desire to do anything. Just as Barton had questioned his purpose in life, I doubted everything about myself.

The bitterness of the winter seeped through my skin, and I felt completely hopeless.

Around New Year's however, I don't know why entirely, but I remember telling Barton, "We need a new routine. I need to do something different."

I went out, bought a dry erase board, and hung it on our kitchen wall. We began to fill it with what we wanted the mornings and evenings to look like, what we needed for ourselves each week, our work and our personal goals.

Every morning, we would sit at the breakfast table and look at the board, with tangible steps and goals. Even if I couldn't get to everything, I would choose one item to accomplish that day. This gave me a focus and grounding point, from which to act.

Slowly, I began making connections with our neighbors, participated in a writer's group and a woman's networking group closer to our home. Making these connections gave me a sense that I was creating a network that we could call upon, depending on the type of support we needed.

I realized that I could not expect one group to provide all the different aspects of support we needed, but instead I began creating connections with many different groups, looking at the ways in which those communities could fill specific roles.

I had been in survival mode for so long. Even before meeting Barton, I had survived two dramatic losses, a broken engagement and my mother's passing, back to back so that I didn't know what real living felt like. With the culmination of all of our experiences of jobs, finances, taking care of the house, realizing we would not have a family in the way we thought—I was worn out.

I could have left Barton. It would have been easier, but I couldn't. There was a reason I stayed. I knew, underneath it all, there was an internal aspiration that I could not grasp.

One piece of this was tangible: when people saw Barton and me together in moments where our love for each other shone through, people were somehow changed by this.

For example, at a benefit event, Barton asked me to dance as an orchestra band was playing. Barton stood and held me in his arms. We looked into each other's eyes and jived to the music. Afterwards, we were standing on the side of the dance floor.

A woman came up to us, "I just wanted to come up and tell you how wonderful you two are to each other. You could just tell that you both are in love. It really affected me. You two are very special."

We thanked her and looked at each other, smiling. Moments like this, we can't create by force; they just happen naturally. And in some small way, our love has changed and reshaped someone's perspective.

There's also a part that is less tangible, tapping into an internal power I had never believed myself to have. Even as a child, I had looked toward my mother and father to tell me what was right, what to do, and even who to be. For the first time, I was looking into my own soul, what was it I needed to do for myself? What was my personal vision and mission in the world?

Having this new understanding, I returned to training, not as I had before, but in a new way, integrating my perspective with the group's vision.

One afternoon, I wrote a note, letting all of my emotions spill out, the times when I had been hurt and angry, the times when I felt no support, my disappointments and fears. Even though I felt completely vulnerable, I knew I had to write it out, and the experience of sharing my words with friends led to a space of reconciliation.

I began to teach both creative journaling workshops and assisted Barton with teaching workshops for martial arts. Yes, there were places that overlapped, and there were times when I needed to do something different. And that was okay.

I was overjoyed when, because of scheduling conflicts, Barton sat in on one of my journaling classes.

Sharing my work with him, and having him understand this aspect of my life felt refreshing.

Even in my work contracts, I could begin to see when I was giving up my power, feeling an intuition return to my senses. Looking for a new contract, I had an interview that went well, but there was something off. While the company was looking for an answer right away, the closer the time came to making it, I felt physically ill. While Barton and I needed to secure a new contract, I was not able commit to the position; later finding out it was the right decision.

Another aspect of my growth came from connecting with other inter-ability couples who began to contact us. The first inter-ability couple we connected with was on the other side of the country.

"Hi, we are Judy and Ron. We saw your blog. We just wanted to call. We hope it's okay."

I spoke over our speakerphone with Barton giggling in the background, "Yes, it's so nice to talk to another couple."

Ron asked, "How do you get around?"

Barton answered, "I take the bus to meetings, and I walk to places close by."

I asked, "How is it having children? We were told we shouldn't have children. But you seem to manage pretty well."

Judy responded, "It's busy, but they are a lot of fun. We're just like any other family."

Ron laughed, "They love getting into trouble, and we have a lot of fun together."

They showed us pictures of their family, and talked about their own journey. I had not seen how a child had interacted with her father who was in a wheelchair, and in a tangible way, I could begin to dream again.

The veil of my own illusion began to fall, and, there was a sense that we could achieve our dreams.

Coming to a place where I completely trust myself, create my own path, and nurture my needs has brought me to embrace my life more fully, to make detours along the way and stand up for myself in a way I had not ever been able to do before.

A Spring Moment

Quietly as breeze to a mid-summer cheek,
warm, subtle
a cradling hand upon my chest.
The sun's rays, soft to the skin,
dabbles just above the surface—
arm hairs stirring to waltz.

~ S. Barton Cutter, March 2009

Chapter Seventeen

Smoking Buses and Other Travel Tribulations

As diligent as we are about travel logistics, inevitably we find ourselves in the most bizarre situations. Lost luggage, highway wreck ahead, bus behind schedule are for amateurs. Wheelchair stuck on the bus lift, bus catching on fire, wheelchair runs out of battery power three miles from home at midnight, plane hit by lightning and losing power, twelve hours of driving in torrential storms with tornado warnings going off on both the departure and arrival, our fifth year anniversary spent in a Nor'easter on a flooded out island—now these are things to write home about.

Admittedly, I am a type A personality, planning details, deadlines, and timelines for every second of the day, and while I have been working to let some of these patterns subside, there is nothing that gets me more tightly wound than traveling. Barton, who seems to come home with these harrowing stories with a nonchalant, how-was-your-day-oh-mine-was-fine attitude, puts me over the edge.

Take the smoking bus for example. I had been organizing a fall festival, and came home from a busy day of working on logistics. I was in the kitchen making dinner. I knew Barton was trekking across town for a meeting. Barton came in; he was standing by the door to the foyer, when I asked how his day was.

Without hesitation and in a vocal tone no more different than boring, how was yours, he said, "Oh, the bus was smoking and we had to get off."

I stopped, hanging on words—the bus was smoking—trying to put the puzzle pieces together and not exactly knowing how they fit.

"What do you mean the bus was smoking?" I squinted my eyes and furled my eyebrows together.

"The bus started filling up with smoke, and..."

Here, my eyes open to the size of golf balls, "The bus caught on fire? Are you okay?"

Barton was laughing at me because he was standing in front of me, so obviously he was okay.

"What happened? The bus caught on fire?" For the rest of the day, there was nothing but talk about how the bus filled with smoke and caught on fire.

Later, at the event I had organized, I was talking with a vendor. "Can you believe it? I was on the bus with Barton, and wow, it was wild. The lift wouldn't work, and the firemen had to pull him and the wheelchair off. Is he okay?"

Again, the squinted brow protrudes on my forehead—fireman had to pull him off. A new piece of information I was now inserting into the picture in my head. Barton never told me about the stuck lift or firemen.

In front of them, I laugh it off, "Oh, he's fine. I couldn't believe it though when he told me the bus was filling up with smoke!"

I'm thinking, "Firemen had to pull him off. Are you serious? I'm going to kill him. But he's home and alive, so I won't kill him, this time. He should know better than not to tell me what happens. If he doesn't want me to hover over him, then give me some credit. I can handle it."

I am learning not to freak out over every little incident. I know he doesn't want me to worry, so he doesn't tell me half the things that happen.

On the day of the fall festival, I had been up before dawn and on my feet all day. Since Barton had just charged his new motor wheelchair, he decided to take the bus to see me in action, and it also meant a three-mile walk when he got off the bus. That night, he wanted to do something special for me, so he carried me in his wheelchair to a local restaurant a few miles away.

Everything was fine, except when Barton's wheelchair began going slower, and the battery indicator began blinking. We were closer to the restaurant than home, and there wasn't a bus running so late. We decided to keep on going and figure out how to get home after dinner.

Although, I went into hyper-overdrive, "What are we going to do? Barton, it's ten pm, how are we going to get home? There's no way I can push you three miles at midnight."

"Look, let's just get there and have dinner. You did a phenomenal job today, and you deserve to celebrate. This doesn't have to spoil our evening. Just let it go, and we'll figure if out later. It'll be okay, I promise."

I was too exhausted to care at that point. We at least arrived at the restaurant and enjoyed a meal and drinks. After we ate, Barton was figuring out plans on what we could do. There was a hotel behind the restaurant. "Why don't we get a room at the hotel and make a romantic evening out of it?"

"How are we going to charge the battery? We still don't have a way to pick it up, unless I walk all the way home by myself and drive back." I was still in panic mode.

"I'm not letting you walk by yourself after midnight. Call Annette, she's right next door and she has a key. Have her pick up my charger, and bring it to the hotel. It's only five minutes away by car, not a big deal."

However, I did feel a little embarrassed for asking our neighbor to bail us out and drive to the hotel with Barton's battery charger. Still, I picked up the phone to call her.

"I'm so sorry to disturb you. I know, it's so late, but I have a huge favor to ask you. Barton's wheelchair ran out of battery power, and we're stuck at a hotel. Can you run by the house and grab the battery charger for Barton's wheelchair so we can plug it in overnight and get home tomorrow? It's on the floor in the bedroom."

Unfortunately this would not be the last time I called our neighbor opening the conversation with "I have a huge favor to ask you."

There was nothing we could do but go with the flow, and so we enjoyed ourselves at a hotel less than three miles from our house. The next morning, we ate breakfast at the hotel, and walked home to feed our dogs and make sure they were okay while we were gone.

The last few weeks had been enough to take the wind out of me, and I was still recovering, but the night at the hotel, that was a fun mini-vacation.

For the longest time, I had trouble understanding why when I spoke of some of the situations that I get myself into, people have such a hard time understanding why I even bother doing it. For me, dealing with getting soaked in the rain, nearly avoiding being hit by a car whose driver isn't paying attention or figuring out how to steer my wheelchair in such a way that I avoid flipping over on the side of a hill seems relatively normal to me.

No, I'm not saying I do these things intentionally, or even on a regular basis; they just seem to be a normal aspect of trying to navigate the world in which we live. Sure, there is a tendency for those who don't know me well to wonder why I would subject myself to such danger. Perhaps they assume because of my disability, I should be sheltered from outside dangers.

But, the world itself is not necessarily a safe space, and it is hard for anyone, even the most skilled athlete to face the world without some element of danger.

When Megan and I first got married, she never expected that I may face some unexpected challenges while out walking around from day to day. The first time I came home laughing about how I managed to avoid flipping my chair over while passing under a bridge on my way to a meeting, she just about flipped her lid. Not in anger, mind you, but out of surprise and fear for my well-being.

My typical response, however, was, "No big deal, any more than a person driving a car may be cut off by someone else on the road. Sure, you may have a moment or two of panic, but you move on and after a few minutes, you realize it was no big deal."

For me, one of the most important points was how I negotiated situations successfully, making it to my destination unscathed. This was difficult to recognize for Megan because she was focused on the potential danger.

After a few times of getting reactions like this, I wondered if it was in fact necessary for me to tell her all of these stories. I tried for a while after this not to tell her some of the things I faced.

Over time, however, I missed sharing these experiences with her because they were a source of liberation, allowing me to understand my own resourcefulness.

I choose independence. With this choice comes the need to be open and able to respond to whatever I may face throughout the day.

I also found as I began to share these stories with Megan, she took on a new appreciation for how I viewed the world in which we lived and my own experience of reality.

There are times when I can appreciate Megan's perspective when it comes to some of the predicaments I get myself into.

Megan often laughs at how I refer to an incident of nearly getting hit by a semi while trying to cross the street, and how it seems not to faze me, but only appeared as a minor facet in a greater story I am trying to tell her. No, her panic, when she hears this, has not entirely dissipated. However, over time, it seems that she has begun to trust the same resourcefulness that I have always relied upon.

My sense of direction is intuitive, and I rarely get lost. Several years ago, when I was coming home from a business meeting, I traveled halfway by bus, deciding to walk the rest of the way. The day was beautiful, and I couldn't bear the thought of transferring onto another bus for the second leg.

That evening when Megan and I were watching TV, we learned on the news that the bus which I would have been on, had I continued on the same bus route, had fallen into a sink hole not far from our house, and those on it had to be evacuated.

I laughed when I heard this, knowing my ability to make a clear judgment of what was needed in the moment had brought me home safely.

We sat in an embrace, forehead to forehead looking into each other's eyes. A scene from *Titanic* flashed before my eyes with a couple embracing, succumbing to their impending deaths.

Barton and I whispered "I love you" over and over while the lights and power flickered and an alarm buzzed. Three to four times, the power faltered before becoming stable again.

The pilot's voice crackled over the intercom. "Ladies and gentlemen, we have received word that there is bad weather in Dallas. The Dallas airport has been shut down for the last hour. We have been circling Dallas for the last fifteen minutes. We have about eight minutes before we will look at options to divert to another airport."

When we emerged from the clouds, the alternative airport looked like a poorly erected Lego construction with battery-operated runway lights. Two personnel stood outside in the rain to direct five planes, twice the size of the terminal.

As the lights came up in the cabin, and the seat belt sign was turned on, the harmonic tone of passengers turning on their cell phones provided a transparent ring of joy throughout the cabin.

We idled on the runway, waiting for the storm to pass; outside a string of other airplanes lined up in front and behind us. An hour later, we weren't moving.

I whispered to Barton, "We're not leaving."

The pilot announced, "Well, there were two planes that took off before us trying to make it to Dallas. However, the storms were just too rough on the planes. They were diverted to another airport north of us. Air traffic control is working on another flight plan that will bring us hopefully south so that we can make it into Dallas. We should be off the ground shortly."

When we did get off the ground, we were flying through what appeared to be a monsoon with torrential rain and wind. I looked out the window to see four-fingered lightning streak across the sky and fall to the earth like fireworks. Normally, such an incredible light show would have brought us immense excitement from each flash; at that moment, it only succeeded in scaring us out of our minds.

Descending into Dallas, the skies were clear. As the tips of the wheels touched the runway, everyone began clapping and cheering.

We watched the last passengers scoot between the aisle and off the plane when the pilot walked down the aisle. Behind him, a man brought in the silver aisle chair.

The pilot said to the co-pilot, "That's what they pay us the big bucks for."

I replied, "Yea, that was a rough trip."

The pilot continued, "I was all right with being hit by lightning and the generator going out on us. But the problems with the landing gear, that was where it got rough."

We walked out into a sea of hundreds of people, and after hours of standing in line, on the phone, we succumbed to the fact that we would be spending the night in the airport. We picked a spot between two waiting areas. I pushed Barton's wheelchair aside so I could lay him on the ground. We stuffed our backpacks under our heads for safekeeping, although I didn't sleep at all.

We spent the next two days in the Dallas airport desperately trying to get back home on stand-by. Each time I would race Barton from one terminal to another, chasing flight after flight, becoming exhausted, irritated, and frustrated as we saw our names move further down on the stand-by list. I would make my way up to speak with the flight representative to explain how we would need an aisle chair, but we never made it that far. If we had, I would have dragged him into his seat myself just to get home. Instead we saw flight after flight take off without us.

In the end, our only solution was to fly to Chicago then transfer to a flight that would take us to Raleigh. After three days of wearing the same clothes, of hauling Barton up and down three airport terminals, I didn't care. It took us three days to fly home, and our luggage arrived two days later.

Again, we survived the unexpected.

Humid

Succulent grey, like the medaling arches where
back and thigh meet,
you call, moist breathed, exposing
the nape of a storm-
silver scented minglings of vapor and convection,
quicken through wet fraying linen.

Honeysuckle pearls slap the earth-
discarded garments of a forgotten evening
still winking lust. The drip of my
bone-soaked longing draws a soul to taste
freshness as you saunter past.

~ S. Barton Cutter, May 2010

Chapter Eighteen

Ink in the Wheels

I never really expected to have a career in the disability field. My ambitions growing up were always to write or edit for major magazines or some large publishing house. But after graduating college, I spent months applying for jobs in marketing, public relations and journalism to no avail.

When I got married however, the responsibilities that I willingly accepted for my wife and family took on new meaning. With it came a new set of priorities that took precedent over the need to follow my own desires.

Once Megan and I moved to North Carolina, I decided to take whatever job possible. The thought crossed my mind that a disability related organization might be a good fit.

From my own life experience, I was aware that service providers were in constant need of committed employees, and having spent years already managing my own direct support work force, I thought surely I could use these skills to help ensure a higher quality of support for other people in similar situations.

I began responding to job listings from various disability organizations in addition to doing a set of cold calls and blind submissions.

"Hello, this is Barton Cutter. I'm calling for a phone interview with Mrs. Christine Schulster."

"Hello? Hello?"

"Yes, my name's Barton. I'm calling for Mrs. Christine Schulster."

"Excuse me?"

"Is Mrs. Schulster in?"

"Sir, are you drunk?" she barked.

I'm appalled and my entire body spasms in anger. "No ma'am. I have Cerebral Palsy. Is Mrs. Schulster available?"

"I'm sorry, sir. Prank calls are horribly inappropriate for a man your age. Goodbye." Click.

This and other similar experiences led me to explore ways to circumvent the language barrier I was facing without drawing direct attention to my disability. I began adding subtle disclaimers in my introductory emails and cover letters mentioning my thick accent, in hopes this would offer those on the receiving end enough advanced warning to invite them into a state of patience and deep listening.

I found the more organizations I called, the more it was apparent that everyone assumed I was in need of services rather than calling on them as a professional in the hopes of offering my skills and unique perspectives within this area.

After perhaps six months of calling organization after organization, I stumbled upon a list of executives. Again, I began inquiring by phone and through submitting my portfolio blindly to those at the CEO level.

One afternoon, I called a local disability provider that had a number of job openings that fit my qualifications.

"Hi, I'm Barton Cutter. I'm interested in speaking with Jason Jacobs to arrange an informational interview."

"Yes, Martin, and what services would you be interested in receiving?"

"Oh, no. I don't need any services. I'm interested in arranging an informational interview with Mr. Jacobs, if possible," I said smiling.

"So you're requiring help with employment, is that correct?"

"Um, not exactly. I'm not interested in receiving services. I am interested in discussing employment opportunities with Mr. Jacobs, if he is available to meet." I tried to disguise my growing irritation under a polite and professional demeanor.

"I'm sorry, I'm not sure I understand. You're not interested in services, is that correct?"

I perked up hopeful that the receptionist was beginning to understand my request, "Yes, it is. I would like to arrange a meeting with Mr. Jacobs, if possible."

"If you're not interested in services, I'm not sure we would be of any help to you. Thank you, and have a good day."

Having found myself continually flustered by my unsuccessful attempts to build connections over the phone, I discovered the initial doorway into my professional career by allowing my writing to speak for itself. In turn, this allowed me, under the right circumstances, to bypass the phone barriers and connect with individuals face-to-face, the medium in which I truly perform the best.

After a few weeks of this newly discovered approach, my portfolio ended up in the hands of a leader in the North Carolina disability field who also shared a particular affinity with well-crafted writing. Through this connection, she became a mentor and a strong advocate for my skills and abilities among other professionals. With her support, I settled into a job for a state organization writing public relations and professional communications material in an eight to five job.

I had always touted this as my dream. It had all the qualities that defined stability and ensured I would be able to provide for my family while engaging many of my strongest talents.

Initially, my role in this particular organization allowed me to explore the impact my writing could have in changing the perspective about those with disabilities in the broader community.

Within the first six months, I produced internal and external marketing material including newsletters, reports, two articles featured in state newspapers and a third that was published in a national disability journal. I was able to secure a marketing campaign increasing the organization's visibility by nearly half a million people. Building relationships with other local disability organizations, I developed a foundation for a personal network of contacts throughout North Carolina.

I soon found, however, the unexpected drawbacks were far more detrimental than I could have ever anticipated. For an inherently outgoing soul, spending my days at the keyboard with limited human interaction, what I had always known as an extremely vibrant world slowly turned to gray without my noticing.

Though much of my job focused on building relationships between organizations, the vast majority of actual interactions occurred through email, and while those with whom I was in contact grew into strong professional allies, I found my time spent in the presence of others dwindling. Initially, I was in the office once a week, but as I became more comfortable with my role, I was given more and more autonomy. With this, there was a decreasing need to come into the main office. Instead, I worked exclusively from my home office, and I soon lost a sense of camaraderie with my co-workers.

Being quiet all day and caught up in my own thoughts led me to talk less in general, and I even became more quiet in other areas of my life. I stopped talking to Megan or to my friends at martial arts training. My curiosity with life's interactions faded, and I found myself isolated and uninterested in sharing and exploring ideas in conversation with friends and family.

Clearly as the colors of my surrounding environment dimmed, with them my passion for the written word faded. After five years in this work, I knew a great deal of my survival depended upon a renegotiation of how I contributed to my community.

"Megan, sit down, we need to talk."

Uh, oh. Barton never began a conversation like this, ever, ever. My mind poured through imaginary scenarios of the unknown. Just like in the moment after Barton told me we were moving to North Carolina or the funding on a contract had been cut. What could possibly be next? I sat on our futon in the living room, bracing myself for the worst.

"Megan, I don't want to ever write again," came from his shaky, almost inaudible voice. "I don't find any joy or passion in it anymore. My passion is connecting with people face to face, and sitting in front of the computer all day just drains me."

Inside I was laughing, and I almost let out a giggle. That was it? Really? Shew, my fears subsided. Still, I could tell how important this was for him. It was a defining moment in our relationship and for him personally.

I listened intently as he described how he didn't want to be a full-time writer anymore, and he wanted to work with people instead. He apologized over and over, though he really didn't need to.

I could tell he was nervous about my reaction, since the love of words and poetry forged the beginning of our relationship and was such a strong part of our story.

I looked Barton in his eyes; I wanted him to hear me. "Barton, I love you for who you are, and it's okay that you don't want to write anymore. I want you to be happy, and if you find yourself doing something else, then I hope you find what you love to do. I love writing, but I don't blame you if you find something else you love."

"Really? You're okay with that?"

"Sure, if you can still write me love poetry. But I understand how isolating it can feel sitting at your computer all day. It's okay if you need to find something else that makes you happy."

I noticed an immediate relief in Barton, and in the weeks that followed, Barton kept his position, but began exploring other ways he could impact families in different and more direct ways. I could see Barton's excitement about life begin to return as he explored new avenues to work in the community.

Several months later, one of our colleagues was writing her last column for the local newspaper, a rotating column that focused on different lives in the community. She urged Barton to apply for the next round of writers.

Though just months earlier he had told me he never wanted to write another word again, he sent in his submission piece:

Getting the Job Done

As I headed to my first job interview, drops of heavy rain smacked my head. I wheeled my power chair out of the apartment complex toward the bus stop. The focus needed to calm my spasticity in the chilling damp combined with the excitement of the day tested my capacity to control my body no matter its state.

Rounding the corner, I shot past a busy parking lot, circumvented a collision and skidded to a halt at the bus stop just in time.

The bus pulled up as the rain increased. The door opened and from the undercarriage, where a wheelchair lift typically deploys, came a horrendous grinding noise.

"The lift ain't working," the driver called out. "I'll call someone to pick you up."

"How long?" I asked.

"Half an hour to forty-five minutes. Find somewhere to get out of the rain."

Pressed for time, I stared at him stunned. There was no way I was leaving the bus stop. What if I missed whomever he was sending?

Despite others' assumption that my life is somehow more challenging with Cerebral Palsy, and that I should behave as such, I was determined to prove otherwise no matter the cost!

An hour passed. I began wondering when I should call the hiring manager.

A white mini-van with a CAT insignia pulled up. In 15 minutes I was there.

Soaked, I greeted my interviewer. Smiling she said, "You could have rescheduled."

"Oh, it's just water!" I laughed.

I was cleaning up the kitchen when I heard Barton in his office. At first, I couldn't tell if he was screaming, laughing, or both. I rushed to his office. Barton's hands were flailing around his head, and he was standing straight up on his foot pedals in front of his computer.

"I got it!" I looked at his computer screen to the email from the editor of our local newspaper accepting him as a rotating columnist.

Through congratulatory hugs and kisses, I was flabbergasted; this was the first time I had seen pure joy and delight in years.

Barton wrote a monthly column for just over a year. Each month, I saw Barton's love of coaching through writing intensify. There were times when I helped, but I was only allowed to transcribe his words verbatim. I had to keep edits or comments to myself, even if he was sharing a story that included me.

Though his column-year has now ended, the goal of 500 words a day remains on the kitchen white-board where we list our daily and yearly intentions.

There is a sense of freedom in owning our writing, editing and coaching business. Challenges along the way ebb and flow while we are working on current contracts while looking for new positions.

While Barton was exploring coaching and mentorship—specifically for youth, parents and families—a transformation was taking place within me as well. It began when I found a website that focused on the connections between writing and wellness. I had just missed their annual conference, so instead, I poured over author names, books and resources that focused on this sub-genre of writing.

Overnight, I realized that I had found it. What I had been searching for my entire life, the place where I fit into the picture. As a child, I didn't have a voice, and many times my stories were cut short. "What is it to help others discover and find their own voice?" I pondered.

I immersed myself in this subgenre that looked at the physiological benefits of creative journaling and writing, and I began teaching workshops on writing after loss, creative journaling, telling your own story and other related topics.

I began exploring how I could enter this world of writing and wellness, should I teach at schools, host workshops, speak at conferences? Over the course of a year, I immersed myself in building a private writing and wellness practice by teaching workshops in all kinds of formats.

At times I could become daunted with the over-saturation of writers hosting workshops, and at other times excited about the ways in which my own writing and coaching could help another through their own life experiences. I began looking at who I wanted to work with, what communities this type of work would benefit and how to reach them.

With each new experience of teaching and working with individuals, I learned insights that were invaluable to a teacher and facilitator. I explored how to create a safe environment for participants to write in and how specific exercises could be helpful for someone writing their own story.

As I explored these communities, I realized an excitement around working with children, youth and adults with disabilities. I could see how for many youth and adults, there isn't an avenue for them to express themselves. Many people assume that because a child can't speak or write they can't communicate.

On the contrary, I have found that visual aide cards, non-verbal expression exercises, telling creative stories, using stories to enhance sensory experiences are ways in which youth with disabilities can explore communication.

Even more profound, many children with disabilities attend moderate or extensive physical therapy, occupational therapy and many other modalities to strengthen physical, behavioral and mental functions. While these therapy avenues are vital and beneficial to the individual as well as the whole family, there is little time left for imaginative play, crucial for childhood development.

In a session with one of my students on my birthday, I received a birthday card that read, "You are a good friend and a good listener. I am smarter because of you. You are quiet and calm. You are fun. You are wonderful."

In a moment of awe, I realized how many people with disabilities don't think they are smart, and how the opportunity to express themselves in whatever way it may be is integral to shifting that perspective.

There have been times when Barton and I are able to work with a family or individual together, using both coaching and writing. We have found that by contributing both of our strengths, we are able to help families shift their perspectives in profound ways.

We also began working and speaking at conferences, both on a local and national level. At one particular conference Barton had organized to empower youth going into higher education, I came to assist with recording and preparing material for speakers.

During lunch, I saw Barton talking with a family on the other side of the reception hall. The mother rested her hand on the side of her son's wheelchair. I caught Barton's eye motioning me to join him.

Barton said, "This is my wife, Megan."

The mother reached over to welcome my hand, and tears welled in her eyes, "Barton has told me how you two met. What a wonderful love story! You are so inspiring, to my son, and to me."

Barton added, "My journey hasn't always been picture-perfect, but I do believe we are all often more capable than we give ourselves credit for."

Barton turned to the son, "And I'm sure if you want to go to college away from home, you and your family will find a way to make that happen. For me, a big part of that has been building a network of friends I can count on."

The young man beamed with excitement. His mother added, "We just get so worried about how he will manage."

I said, "In the time I've known Barton, he's taught me a lot about resourcefulness. There are challenges that we face, sometimes on a daily basis, but somehow we always seem to find a solution."

While I stood on the sidelines to listen to the rest of their conversation, I realized how much concern parents experience for their children over whether they will be able to live fulfilling lives, and the anxiety about allowing their children to experience all of what life holds, both positive and negative experiences.

In working with youth and families, we are mentoring and guiding others to find their own independence and voice. I continue to be amazed at how working with youth and families has inspired me to work harder and share more about our experiences as an inter-ability couple.

Since I have led group writing workshops and individual writing and coaching sessions, in addition to speaking with Barton, my own confidence has grown. I find myself fulfilling one of my dreams, to help others through creative expression.

Both Megan and I had done a great deal of work to figure out where it was that we were called to serve and work. I had returned to martial arts training and in combination with my coaching, had realized that much of my greatest ability to help others lay in serving people with disabilities. The core of my passion focused on how to navigate traditional and non-traditional systems of care while taking responsibility for one's own actions and contribute to the community through one-on-one coaching.

Megan, likewise, continued to clarify and deepen her passion for using writing as a means to enhance self-expression for youth and families with disabilities.

As we moved further into these directions and began to combine Megan's use of writing with my coaching practice, it became evident that we were quickly outgrowing the original establishment of our writing and editing company.

After six years of building our communications business, an idea began to percolate quietly in the back of my mind. I knew at some level an entire rebranding of our company was needed. I also knew what a big step this would be for both of us.

While I was game to venture into this new territory, I knew that Megan would need a little more time to accept the gift of moving into new possibilities, so I approached the subject with caution. I sympathized with her. Just as she feared losing her writing spirit, I had lived through an experience in which my joy of expressing life's extraordinary moments through the poetic had been diminished to the empty repetition of staring at the computer screen day after day.

A transformation such as this would be calling us to abandon the old levels of security that we had found in providing marketing and public relations for small businesses. We would be asked instead to trust in our unique potential as an inter-ability couple. We would discover an unorthodox skill set to reach out and connect to others who have disabilities and offer new opportunities to discover their own empowerment and personal freedom.

At first, I asked nothing more than for each of us to do a personal exercise of writing down our personal mission statements and then extrapolating a cohesive mission and vision for what we wanted our business to become.

After some subtle pushing, Megan and I went out to dinner and discussed what our new business concept would look like. It was not long before I felt her trepidation of stepping into a new realm transform into a pervasive excitement about the potential impact we could have on the lives of others.

We began to examine the ways in which people with disabilities can optimize their independence through balancing traditional supports such as Medicare and Social Security Disability Income with multi-faceted approaches from connecting with friends for support to the exploration of interests and hobbies as a way to build social involvement and find employment.

While I am the type of person who would abandon federal or state supports altogether, for most people, it's too scary because of the reliance on traditional care systems for basic needs such as housing, food and personal care.

Instead, we found that by embracing aspects of the traditional systems, many people are more willing to experiment with other possibilities to meet their needs. These traditional systems have limitations, from defining how much one can earn to how many hours of personal care one is eligible for, and even whether one can legally marry without losing supports.

Balancing on the edge of the box, with one foot using traditional support systems and the other foot exploring other ways to meet one's needs, became a crucial component in how we work with individuals and families touched by disability to embrace a fuller and more cohesive life.

From this, our new business name, Cutter's Edge Consulting emerged and with it, the hallmark image of walking along the edge of a mountain toward one's freedom.

However, it would be another three months before I was able to get Megan to the point of allowing me to file the paperwork for the legal name change for our company, and once this was done, we began the tedious endeavor of rebranding our entire business model.

As fall came, we were working on our website which was completed except for a few pages, at a local coffee shop. Megan suddenly exclaimed, "We need to stop writing and start doing something."

I was knocked flat on my face by hearing her words. She now was fully on board recognizing it was time we step up our efforts.

Within three days, we had researched local disability events and had signed ourselves up for several over the next six weeks. Our heads were reeling with excitement. There was still so much to do.

Marketing materials had to be created, and we got them out in a flash. After each event, we evaluated what worked and what didn't, and we began to look at new ways to reach those we hoped to work with more directly.

Many times, people with disabilities have been trained not to dream because they are surrounded by lowered expectations, unintentionally creating a paradigm that limits the vision of what their life could be like.

From a very early age, parents are inundated with advice, professional opinion and social pressures, dictating to them what their child can and cannot do or be. Parents face a barrage of emotional challenges as well, and can sometimes fall into the disappointment of losing their own dreams for their children. What will their child's life be like now? Rather than getting their hopes up for what their child's life might be like despite disability, they stop daring to envision possibilities.

For example, many parents ask their children what they want to be when they grow up. Firemen, astronauts, or veterinarians. Or parents may see their child love baseball or ballet, and so they guide them and give them more training.

Yet, many children with disabilities aren't asked about what they want to be when they grow up. Instead, there seems to be a quiet expectation that for people with disability, particularly when the disability is severe, a mainstream profession is out of reach.

Similarly, professionals have a responsibility to be realistic and may not want to give false hope, because they are trying to protect parents as well as themselves. Professionals in the disability arena face a high burn out rate, and though they may care deeply for the families they serve, they may not have the energy to dedicate the time required to hold a high level of success for every family. Day after day, they see families struggling with all of the challenges that a family faces. And so they too, aim for the most minimal of expectations.

Of course, surrounded by this mentality, the person, whether a child or adult with a disability, becomes acculturated to this belief. Our work involves helping youth and adults with disabilities as well as their families unlearn this conviction. Regaining their own capacity and courage to dream serves as a fundamental building block for success, self-reliance, resilience, and confidence.

In addition to one's ability to dream, learning from mistakes is an equally invaluable developmental skill. Few opportunities offer us the greater chance to learn than the times in life where we fail. Not only do these moments allow us to problem solve, but over time, these skills help us to manage disappointment and gain the resiliency to try again.

In my experience, there are two common patterns that emerge. Among parents of people with disabilities, it's not uncommon to become over-protective, viewing their own child as uniquely susceptible to life's dangers. In these situations, every attempt is made to shelter a child from any occurrence, believing that it is better to shield against all negative possibilities.

At the other extreme, other parents may push too hard, wanting their child to succeed at all costs. This overcompensation may at times harden the child or youth to take a rigid view of what is acceptable and become unwilling to explore anything outside of their parent's view.

In my own experience growing up, I was fortunate enough to have parents who encouraged me to explore beyond my comfort zone. And except for the occasional hard-nosed challenge that was deemed "for my own good," they were receptive to how I interpreted and explored my needs.

For example, at age of four, I returned from a day at camp where one of the older campers had been using her new power wheelchair. At one point, she recognized my intrigue and offered me the opportunity to sit in her lap and take the chair for a spin. I was hooked. The freedom to move independently was so freeing and I knew, even at that young age, that this could open up worlds for me.

That evening at home, I said to my parents, "I need a wheelchair with one of those gear things so I can make it go on my own."

They recognized immediately what I was saying as well as my desire and motivation to be able to navigate my world independently. Amazingly, I was fitted for a wheelchair and as soon as I got myself into the seat, I was tearing off about the house trying to fit into the tiniest places in order to learn the limits of my newfound tool.

With coaching and mentorship, we learn how to accept mistakes and failure for what they are: an opportunity for learning and growth, rather than a reason to shut down and give up.

We show our clients, both individuals and organizations, how to enjoy small successes and build on these to achieve their visions.

By doing so, our clients learn how to persevere through negotiating life's challenges and move through their own fears.

Rich is the damp that hangs from the eve-
a crystallizing resin sweet
with the nectars of myth.　W
The yawing creak of a rocking chair
echoes softly in the silence of August grey.

Flannel's bristle and sap of
aged Maxwell House
keep vigil-
armed sentinels holding fast against
a rising chill.

~ S. Barton Cutter, August 2009

Chapter Nineteen

The Waves, a Mountain, and a Breath of Fresh Air

Out of the back of the ferry, we watched a pair of sea hawks gliding on the airstream of the boat. Above them, the first blue sky in five days. We were unprepared for such an eventful week filled with the howling winds, hurricane rains and ten-foot ocean swells.

As we were planning for our fifth year anniversary vacation to Hatteras Island, the weather forecast was sunny and calm, with some talk of storms forming in the middle of the Atlantic with a projected course far south of us. We packed for a week away from home, even bringing our dogs with us, filling a rented accessible van so Barton could be in his motor wheelchair for the week.

Not only were we celebrating a milestone in our marriage, we had also hoped to spend the week writing, creating some fun videos and finding ways to get Barton's coaching practice off the ground.

Arriving at our rented beach house, the main living area on the fourth floor, we were awed at how we could watch the ocean surf from the front porch and turn around to see the calm sound off of the bedroom veranda.

For two days we basked in the reflection of the sound, where the horizon merged into a mingling of sky and water.

On our anniversary, we drank champagne with strawberries, read poetry, and danced to music. We sat on the porch swing reflecting on the last five years of unexpected adventures, making for a rich and diverse life together, and we dreamed of our future together, wondering what was to come.

While we were absorbed in our own celebrations, we heard reports of a Nor'easter blowing into Hatteras, but disregarded them as insignificant. The power went out the first night of the storm, and as we looked down the street, we realized it wasn't just our rental house. In the morning, the power flickered as it came back on.

The next morning, I took the rental van to higher ground, leaving it in the parking lot by the post office. On the walk back to the house, I found a little gas station open where I stocked up on food items. There was a point where scurrying to prepare dissipated, and I succumbed to enjoying this unfamiliar situation.

However, when the force of the wind moved the entire house, rattling the mirror clock on the bedroom wall, I was quite unsettled. Despite my nerves, we remained inspired by nature's breathtaking power in the surge of the ocean waves.

Witnessing the power of the water crashing onto the shore and listened to the constant wind across the ocean, we watched dolphins flip through the incredible surf. Storm clouds moved across the sound, and we caught a faint rainbow between downpours. That night, however, the clouds opened up, and we cuddled in sweatshirts watching the stars shimmer across the night's sky.

Later in the week, we ventured out to Hatteras Village and realized how lucky we were. Water covered nearly all of the streets, and all of the shops were closed.

We stopped at the only restaurant that we could find open, and pulled into a gravel parking lot, still brimming with rainwater.

Eating fried shrimp and a fish sandwich, we listened to locals talk about damage to the main road.

To get off the island, we had to take ferries to the mainland because the road north of us had been washed out. Before sunrise on our last day, I stepped out of our beach house and watched a long line of cars heading to the ferry. Less than an hour later, we too pulled onto the watery roads to evacuate. We passed several cars where water had engulfed their entire hoods.

When we approached the ferry dock, the waters rose higher against the side of the van. I began hyperventilating.

"Just a little further, we can do it," I gasped.

The battery light was blinking, and my heart raced. We weren't going to make it. I looked with terror at Barton, who was laughing, in his typical Barton response. What were we going to do, turn around?

There was no heading back, only forward.

We pulled up behind a string of cars, vans and trucks waiting to board the ferry. Since I was still in a panic over the battery light, I asked a woman if they knew how the roads were on the other side and if we could follow them in case anything happened.

We were excited to learn we had found another family, who were in the pre-stages of adoption. Right away the tension of the drive to the ferry dock melted away, and we began to ask questions about the process of adoption and what to look for in purchasing our own accessible van.

For me, this was one of the first couples I had met who allowed me to see adoption as a real possibility. I felt comfort in being able to ask questions I normally didn't talk about with other people because of preconceived assumptions. I was elated to be able to ask questions without having to educate someone else about life as an inter-ability couple, or to justify why we would want to have a child, just like any other family.

As an inter-ability couple, we've had many challenges along the way from people who thought we shouldn't be married in the first place to a continual break down of stereotypes where a family member has a disability. But with laughter and a bit of perseverance, we have walked through many of those challenges. We've also had many joys in our marriage, from eating Chinese take-out on the floor of our first house to reading and speaking at many different conferences and events. We were always a part of something new and exciting. We are always amazed at the different projects we have worked on over the years.

Barton and I arrived on the mainland of the North Carolina coast, disoriented from having to take an unexpected route home. I had no idea where we were, but we set off trusting our GPS system. We soon found this wasn't much help, arriving at a detour sign that pointed down a road, covered by waters flooding houses on either side. We laughed at the absurdity and reveled in our mutual love for the adventure.

Our fifth-year anniversary was one we would talk about for years to come.

There is something sacred in the small gifts of time that Megan and I have given to one another over the past eight years. They appear like erupting stars from the depths of the universe to offer us moments of respite from the crazed madness that we often find ourselves in, managing work and home, training and family. Within these breaks, we return to the same sources of inspiration that originally beckoned us to delve into the unending adventure of day-to-day life.

Since we first married, we often treat each other to the journeys that eventually lead us to reconnect with the most fundamental aspects of who we are. These journeys come in many forms. Extended vacations offer a retreat from the outside world and give us space to reflect the admiration we have for each other. Other brief moments in the mid-stream of our busy lives open a syncopated pause, and we find ourselves grateful to rediscover a playful joy that inspires us to carry on.

Each year, my family retreats to the woods of New Hampshire to pause, enjoy a breath of fresh mountain air, and listen to the deep silence that bespeaks the mountains, indeed a tradition far older for me than visiting the waters. I've been fortunate enough to be born into this family where, for five generations now, we have been the perennial inhabitants of that peaceful land, the place where I have come to know myself, my family and perhaps most importantly, a profound and unending connection with nature.

Over the past thirty-some years that I have ventured to the great White North, my connection to it has evolved as my appreciation for what it has to offer reveals itself in unending layers. Growing up, I was a member in a family whose most common pastime was to take off by foot into these mountains and learn trail by trail the love that my great grandfather originally felt when he came to map these lands. It was difficult at times, to be the only person unable to journey with them, and it would take me time to appreciate how these woods would one day grow an independent connection for me.

With time, it grew indeed, and while cousins tramped up to explore the peaks that surrounded Randolph Valley, I discovered the subtle joys that were found in the silence of the woods, alongside ancient glacial streams, and the connections between life in the valley and the ever vigilant granite ridges above.

When I first met Megan, I dreamed immediately of introducing her to this magical land which I called home, though I rarely spent more than a week or two there each summer. I knew, somehow, that the way she would receive this place would indicate to me just how sustainable our love might become.

Indeed, as I had hoped, the first time we travelled to those mountains as a couple, she fell in love with them immediately, and this in turn, increased our connection to one another more than I had anticipated.

It wasn't until years later, however, that we both began to recognize the significance of how this land supported us as a couple through the magic it quietly offered year by year.

There were several seasons during which we were unable to return for various reasons. At the time, we thought little of it, for we had become so involved in our daily lives that the peace we found there had slipped from our lives, like one who is never missed until his absence is pointed out. Shortly after I returned from the edge of my own uncertainties, we returned to those mountains to honor the passing of one of my closest cousins.

The afternoon we arrived, Megan and I walked down to the brook that cuts through the backyard of my father's field, and I asked Megan to help me out of my wheelchair to sit on the earth for a while. It was there, in that silence and peace of the moment that I at once allowed the fullness of the valley life to pour back into my soul. I sat still for hours upon the bank feeling the soft earth, moss and grass beneath my feet while Megan dabbled in the brook, taking pictures of the quiet and often overlooked wildlife.

We recognized how vital and nurturing this land had become for the two of us, and we knew not a year could pass without us at least visiting, in brief, to inhale the crisp white air and gaze upon the softened faces of the Presidential Peaks.

Each year that we have returned since, our gratitude and connection has deepened, and with it, new understanding of what the relationship to these places signifies. It is here indeed, that Megan reminds me to reconnect with the quiet strength of the mountain peaks that have for so long taught me to stand in my own way.

After seven years of marriage, we sat in rocking chairs on the back porch overlooking the valley that we have come to know as home. As we rocked, I was reflecting on how far we had come and close we felt.

I felt myself falling in love with Megan all over again, but it was different; once again, we just fit together. For the first time in many years, I felt this way, and I couldn't imagine not being intertwined in our partnership. We were both aware of a clear direction, and this made us inseparable.

As the storm came in and met the mountains, the peaks were embraced by the soft folds of the burgeoning clouds, moist with life. With the first rain meeting the quiet layer of the stream's surface, each drop drew my ear's attention deeper into the surrounding silence.

Our eyes met, breath mingling as the coursing of angels remembering wholeness. Above, a red tail spiraled in the thickening rain. The two worlds, flesh and spirit, earth and sky, united in a clap of thunder.

When we reemerged, we moved together into the unfolding of what is yet to come.

In the milk-chocolate glow of late summer,
the warm arch of your neck,
supple like the lingering taste of fresh molasses,
rouses the corners of my tongue like a softening memory
of rosewater.

~ S. Barton Cutter

And the Love Rolls on...

Epilogue

Though the numerous experiences over the last nine years have created many adventures to tell, we are certain our lives will continue to be filled with love, laughter and the thrill of navigating both the bizarre and mundane, as we move deeper into the unknown avenues of our life's work.

The story is left undone. While we have found ourselves coming face to face with the realization of goals that we never anticipated, there are still those dreams that linger on the horizon waiting for us to embrace with full accomplishment as they call us into the world of becoming ourselves.

So inexplicably linked, our work and home life cradle and support one another to offer ourselves in service to others, that they may discover the fullness and beauty of realizing their own dreams. Our prayer is that our work in mentorship, coaching and creative expression can serve as a beacon that guides each person we work with to recognize their own vast potential and find their way safely to its fruition.

The story is not merely our own. We offer our small portion as a companion to your own. The question that calls to us all: who is it that we dream of being and how do we express this moment-by-moment, day-by-day and year-by-year?

We hope our story has inspired you and gives you courage to embrace the truth within your own story, and by doing so, make each moment precious.

Questions to Ponder

Discussion

1. What themes stuck with you most throughout the book?

2. If you were in Barton's position of choosing love and marriage or a safety net of supports, which would you choose and why? How would you make your decision?

3. Both of the families had concerns over Barton and Megan's life together. How would you respond if your child/children found love in an inter-ability relationship? What possibilities or concerns would you see?

4. Why do you think we have so much trouble acknowledging people with disabilities as sexual beings?

5. Compare and contrast the different relationships between the main characters and their parents. What relationships are missing? What questions would you have for the main characters vs. their parents?

6. As you read about Barton's misadventures, do you find yourself wanting to protect him? What would it be like for you?

7. Barton and Megan have moments where they feel they've lost their way. How have you experienced those times, and how do you find your way back?

8. Throughout the book, what development did you see Barton and Megan go through, as individuals, and as a couple?

9. What motivates Barton and Megan, as individuals, and as a couple? And how did this evolve?

10. For Barton, standing and walking his bride down the aisle after they were married was a powerful experience for everyone present. When have you stood for something you believed in and how did it affect others?

11. Megan fell into the trap of listening to other people's opinions. When have you listened to others? How can you listen to your own voice?

12. Some would argue that trying to walk despite the odds is a denial of the situation and/or who one is. Barton did not feel this way. What's your perspective?

13. Both Barton and Megan struggled with how to expand their family after learning they could not have children naturally. What concern, challenges, or questions would you have in their situation? And how would you honor your dream?

14. Courage is a central theme throughout the book. Where and how does courage show up most in your life?

15. Has this memoir shifted your perspective about the human potential? If so, how?

About the Authors

Biography

Barton is a professional coach and mentor who uses his humor and uncompromising wit to empower youth with disabilities and their families to discover a clear and powerful vision of their own independence within the community of their choosing. He combines his life experience of living with Cerebral Palsy and a professional background of youth leadership to support children and families to bring their vision to life through action steps that are both inspiring and practical.

After graduating from The University of Arizona, Barton spent several years spear-heading Youth Leaders in Action, an advocacy and leadership program for junior high and high school age youth with disabilities. Under his direction, Youth Leaders in Action developed a leadership curriculum to empower youth with disabilities to advocate for themselves. Further, he was a driving force behind a statewide conference focused on youth with disabilities and post-secondary education in which he united stakeholders with various interests under a common vision and achieved unified goals.

Barton has also functioned as the Communications Director for The North Carolina Council on Developmental Disabilities and Co-Coordinator for the Lifetime Connections Program with First in Families of North Carolina. From 2011-2012, he was a monthly columnist for The News & Observer Our Lives Column. Today, he continues his work with various organizations while offering coaching and mentoring to private clients.

Megan is a creative writing and expressions facilitator, using writing, visual arts, storytelling and non-verbal expression to support youth and adults of all abilities to tell their powerful story, facilitate communications within a family unit and establish community support networks.

After graduating from Randolph-Macon Woman's College, Megan worked in corporate marketing until 2005 when she began a full-time writing and teaching practice. In addition, she is a writer, social media strategist and online reputational manager for organizations, small businesses and individuals.

Currently, she teaches one-on-one and group sessions to youth, adults and families of all abilities in addition to writing articles for local publications. She is dedicated to providing a space that allows the creative process to evolve in a way that empowers others to recognize their powerful voice and learn how to use it effectively.

Together, they break many barriers and assumptions through being open about their relationship, speaking locally and nationally about disability awareness, inclusionary leadership training, creating healthy relationships, relationships and disabilities, self-defense for people with disabilities and emergency preparedness.

www.inkinthewheels.com

www.cuttersedgeconsulting.com

www.loverollson.com

CPSIA information can be obtained at www.ICGtesting.com
Printed in the USA
BVOW071059280113

311701BV00002B/4/P